COUNTRY

HERBS

TECHNIQUES, RECIPES, USES, AND MORE

COUNTRY
HERBS
TECHNIQUES, RECIPES, USES, AND MORE

KATHI KEVILLE

J. B. FAIRFAX
LONDON

A FRIEDMAN GROUP BOOK

Published 1991 by J B Fairfax Limited
Ferry House, 51/57 Lacy Road
Putney, London, SW15 1PR

By arrangement with Michael Friedman Publishing Group, Inc.

Copyright © 1991 by Michael Friedman Publishing Group, Inc.

ISBN 1 85391 291 3

A catalogue record for this book is available from the British Library.

COUNTRY HERBS
Techniques, Recipes, Uses, and More
was prepared and produced by
Michael Friedman Publishing Group, Inc.
15 West 26th Street
New York, New York 10010

Editor: Sharon Kalman
Art Director: Jeff Batzli
Layout: Helayne Messing
Photography Researcher: Daniella Jo Nilva

Typeset by M&M Typographers, Inc.
Colour separation by Universal Colour Scanning Ltd.
Printed and bound in Hong Kong by Leefung-Asco Printers Ltd.

DEDICATION
Dedicated to my parents, Naomi and Jesse Keville,
who first introduced me to the beauty of nature,
and to Marian Wycoff and Betty Longshore,
for their bountiful encouragement and inspiration.

ACKNOWLEDGMENTS
A heartfelt thank you to my editors,
Sharon Kalman and Al Moak,
who were both a delight to work with.

© Maggie Oster

CONTENTS

YOUR COUNTRY HERB GARDEN

You don't have to live in the country to have a country-style herb garden. In fact, some of the most delightful herb gardens I have seen have been contained in an eight-foot square. Even a planter box or a series of large pots can provide enough space for herb gardening. My first garden held forty different herbs in an eighteen-square-foot plot.

An herb garden will give you pleasure throughout the year. Spring contains the excitement of plants emerging from the earth with bursts of energy. The summer garden is filled with beauty and fragrance. Autumn brings the bountiful harvest. Winter is a time for dreaming and planning and enjoying all of your dried and preserved herbal creations.

HERB GARDEN DESIGN

An exciting facet of herb gardening is the design. This is your chance to be an artist, using nature as your canvas. Nature itself is your assistant, since herbs have a way of creating beauty no matter how they are combined. Still, certain techniques can make your garden especially attractive. The fun in planning is choosing and putting together different elements to create your own unique style.

Country herb gardens are versatile. They can be grown on a terraced slope, in a border wrapped around the side of a house or lawn, and even in pots on your porch or balcony. Basic design for a garden is like any art. You create a contrast in color, texture, and form. The most appealing herb gardens keep your eye moving from bed to bed in visual delight. The herbs themselves offer much to work with.

Design inspiration can come from many sources: a diagram of a traditional herb garden, gardens you visit, and nature. An excellent place to see garden design in action is in established herb gardens. Find them at historical homes, herb nurseries, botanical gardens, museums, herb shops, and private homes. Your visits will help you choose favorite varieties and get a feel for which herbs are best for your particular garden. Local herb and garden societies have a wealth of information about local growing conditions and sources of plants.

Sketch your designs on paper, where they can be easily changed. Once you choose a final plan, lay out the garden with strings tied to stakes so you can walk through and visualize your dream garden. Make sure that pathways are wide enough to allow herbs to trail and bush out into them. Check to see that the herb beds are a convenient size for harvesting.

Herb gardens are for enjoyment, so have fun with them from the beginning. While designing your herb garden, keep in mind that you can always make changes. Even well-established herbs can be moved after they are planted. If you think the tansy has become ungainly, as it tends to, or the pink yarrow might look better next to lavender than it does to sage, dig them up and move them. A small herb garden can always be enlarged and an area overgrown with weeds can be dug up and replanted.

© Derek Fell

© Derek Fell

CHOOSING THE HERBS

A combination of tall- and low-growing herbs create depth and variety in your garden. Tall fennel and angelica, and small trees and bushes such as bay, juniper, and myrtle, add more dimension to your garden. Know how tall and wide your herbs will grow so you are not surprised one day to find the little pennyroyal and sweet woodruff hidden by an overbearing wormwood. The simplest designs place large herbs in a central location or in the back row, then work down in height to the smallest herbs.

Colors can contrast strongly, moving gradually from softer hues to a brighter crescendo, or they can follow the color wheel. Herbal leaf colors range from soft blue-grays to yellow-greens, and they exhibit a variety of textures. Though many herb flowers are small, they often are so numerous that they seem to cover the entire plant. A rambling thyme plant in full bloom looks like a floral carpet. Herbs like echinacea and calendula provide large, bright blooms. Don't hesitate to include the colorful accents of nonherbal flowers, such as daisies, cosmos, bachelor buttons, and zinnias, because they provide additional color for your herbal crafts projects. Even subtle color contrasts can work well if the herbs present a variety of textures. One of herb gardener Aldema Simmons's most famous gardens at Caprilands in Connecticut is filled with gray herbs and gray stone walkways.

DESIGNING THE BEDS

Ideally, herb beds should be narrow enough so you can reach in and harvest what you want without disturbing the garden. If you prefer wider beds, stepping stones can give you easy access to the herbs. Traditionally, many herb gardens were planted in raised beds. The reason was both practical and decorative, since taller beds bring low-growing herbs up to an easy height to pick or smell. Creeping thymes and mints are very pretty growing over the edges of raised beds.

Increase the bed height by moving topsoil to it from path areas or other areas of the garden. Topsoil can also be purchased from nurseries or garden centers. Gently slope the dirt edges, or contain the beds within railroad ties, thick wooden boards (which last about six years, then need replacing), or even the spokes of an old wagon wheel. Brick, cement, or rock walls can also edge beds. In medieval monastic gardens, like the Cloisters Herb Garden of the New York Metropolitan Museum of Art, willow and other flexible branches were woven together to hold the beds. Traditional monastery herb gardens offered gardeners and visitors a raised chamomile bed or a bench to sit upon and enjoy the garden.

Banks overflowing with herbs, sunken areas, and small pools add interesting dimensions to an herb garden. An impressive bank of overgrown lavender and rosemary at the Los Angeles County Arboretum makes the herbs look eight feet tall. This arboretum and also the Stryburg Arboretum in Golden Gate Park, San Francisco, use banks held by rock walls to bring fragrant gardens close to the hands and noses of the blind.

European gardens of the sixteenth century favored herb beds surrounded by hedges of germander, thyme, hyssop, and santolina. These were pruned into square or cylindrical shapes. The most elaborate version was the knot garden, where contrasting herbs, carefully planted and trimmed, gave the impression that they were knotted together. In *The Art of Gardening* (1568), Thomas Hyall wrote that English Tudor knot gardens were made "with hyssop and

© Derek Fell

thyme or with winter savory and thyme for these endure all the winter through green." If you have some spare time (or a hired gardener) to keep the hedges trimmed, you might want to create a knot garden.

Most perennial herb plants do not grow to full size until their third summer. So, when designing your herb garden, keep in mind that initially there will be empty spaces be- tween the herbs. You can temporarily fill this space with other perennials that can later be moved, or with annual herbs or flowers. There are many free-sowing annual and bi- ennial herbs that fill in every available gap year after year. Borage, calendula, German chamomile, foxglove, evening primrose, marigolds, sesame, parsley, or poppies will all be happy to volunteer.

© Maggie Oster

POTTED GARDEN

Any size containers can be placed together to make an herb garden. Old crocks or hollow cinder blocks are interesting pots. Oak barrel halves, available at some nurseries, or planter boxes can hold a collection of many different herbs. Planter boxes can become window boxes, but be sure they are made strong enough to hold the weight of the dirt. Set wooden containers up on bricks or stones so they do not rot. Incidentally, small planters with three or four herbs make wonderful gifts. For instance, you can give a culinary garden of thyme, rosemary, sage, and basil.

Potted herbs also fit into the garden scheme. Traditional English herb gardens often included small potted bay trees and other herbs that are sensitive to the cold. They could be carried into the hot house for the winter. Hanging pots of herbs are always attractive. A number of herbs, in-cluding Persian catnip, trailing rosemary, and ground ivy hang very gracefully. Elizabethans were especially fond of hanging rosemary pots.

Be aware that peppermint, pennyroyal, and other members of the mint family are notorious for their ability to spread throughout the garden. And, they are not the only ones! Other roving herbs include white and pink yarrow, ground ivy, creeping thymes, and perennial clovers. These herbs can work to your advantage to fill in areas, but they need restriction in a small garden. Plant them in enclosures, such as clay pipes, cement bricks, or pots that go down at least six inches if you want to keep their roots contained.

I have seen herb gardens where all the plants are actually in pots buried in the soil. When fall comes, the pots are dug up and placed in a greenhouse. They sprout extra early in the spring and then the entire garden is tilled to eliminate weeds before the pots are again "planted."

Parsley, chives, and tarragon are herb plants every cook will want to keep handy; all three can easily be grown in a pot.

© Maggie Oster

PATHWAYS

Traditional herb gardens were almost always designed in symmetrical squares or circles, accented by pathways. Paths not only look nice, but they are also practical, since they allow easy access into the garden for weeding, harvesting, and, of course, enjoying. Paths can radiate from the center, form concentric circles, or spiral through the garden. Since a country herb garden can also be informal, the path can ramble casually through the plants.

Paths can be constructed from flagstones, cement forms, or bricks set into patterns. Gravel, small rocks, sand, and even sawdust can be set around stepping stones or can form the path itself. One simple garden design sets square cement steps, about two feet wide, in a checkerboard pattern and fills in the space between them with herbs. Level and pack the dirt under the path area to keep down the weeds. Consider laying heavy gauge plastic, tar paper, or even sawdust under the path as a weed barrier. Sand or sawdust between the plastic and the stones increases its life span.

Anyone who strolls down an herb garden path has the pleasure of brushing past a potpourri of scented herbs. You might even allow a few sprigs of these herbs to escape into the path, where they will scent the walk when they're stepped on. In his *Essay of Gardens*, Francis Bacon said the plants that "perfume the air most delightfully . . . when trodden upon are burnet, wild thyme and . . . mint."

Bacon suggested that "whole alleys" of such herbs be planted for pathways and that the entire path be a bed of herbal ground covers. It is a little more work to maintain, since herbs in the bed and path will always be trying to invade each other's territory, but the effect is very herbal. Some herbs tolerate being walked on quite well. For instance, Roman chamomile was one of the most popular plants for the scented lawns of sixteenth-century Europe. Shakespeare's character Falstaff comments that "the more it is trodden upon, the faster it grows or the better it wears."

ACCESSORIES

Herb gardens lend themselves to a variety of decorative accents. Traditional herb gardens include sundials, birdbaths, and even wells filled with plants, usually placed in the center. If you add statuary, consider St. Francis or St. Fiacre, the patron saint of herbs. Signs painted on slate or engraved in wood or metal can identify herbs or display an appropriate saying. You can have fun with accessories, and you can even use them to make theme areas within your garden.

Trellises, supported by sturdy walls and fences, can be filled with flowering vines. Free-standing trellises can also be incorporated into the design. Honeysuckle, roses, clematis, jasmine, and hops are just a few of the climbing plants suitable for your herb garden. Rosemary lends itself to being shaped into elaborate patterns supported on a wall or into a topiary, giving the impression of a miniature tree.

Benches are a thoughtful addition, providing visitors— and the gardener—a place to sit and relax while enjoying the garden. In a small garden, place a bench along one edge. If your garden is large enough, an arbor filled with roses, clematis, or other climbing flowers adds a special touch over a sitting area or to a garden entrance. On a grander scale, a garden gazebo might be incorporated into your garden. This offers a private place to sit and read about herbs while sipping herbal tea from the garden.

© Gay Bumgarner/Photo/Nats

The garden bench offers a resting stop for the weary gardener or the casual visitor to pause and enjoy.

© Maggie Oster

CHAPTER TWO

CULTIVATING YOUR HERB GARDEN

Even if your green thumb seems to be more of a brown shade, don't despair—growing herbs is easy if you know a few tricks. Herbs are naturally wild plants that are very forgiving to even the most inexperienced gardener. Since most herbs have not been hybridized, they are hardy survivors and are quite resistant to drought and insect invasions. In fact, many herbs contain natural pesticides.

Look to the country where the herb's ancestors originate. Duplicating that environment as much as possible will make your herbs feel right at home. Most of our classical cooking and fragrance herbs, such as lavender, rosemary, and thyme, come from the Mediterranean. Although you may not be able to duplicate a Grecian hillside overlooking the Aegean Sea, their native home and climate will provide guidelines for preparing garden soil and watering. These herbs prefer little rain, well-drained soil, and lots of sunshine.

Many of the most popular herbs from other parts of the world adapt well to a Mediterranean-type herb garden. The few exceptions include shade-loving plants, such as sweet woodruff, rosemary, and sage, which prefer to dig their roots into rich, loamy soil. A specially prepared section of your yard will make them completely happy.

SOIL

Let's start with the basics. How is your soil? The old gardening cliché is "poor soil, little water makes strong herbs." Well, only to a point. It is true that over-pampered herbs become less hardy with fewer flowers and less fragrance. Yet, while herbs do not need the rich garden soil tomatoes and corn demand, they do require nourishment.

Mediterranean soil tends to be high in alkaline and well drained. If your garden soil is too acidic, add lime, hardwood ashes, and ground eggshells. How do you know if your soil is acid? Garden supply stores have inexpensive tests available and lots of advice. You can also send a sample of your soil to the local county cooperative extension office for analysis. Most herbs do not like to keep their "feet" wet. A well-drained soil lets water drain down, encouraging roots to search deeply for water and nutrients.

The best fertilizer I have found to improve any type of soil (and I have dealt with quite a few) is a simple organic compost. Even when my garden started out with heavy, red clay soil that seemed better suited for pottery than gardening, compost came to the rescue. Raised beds improved the poor drainage somewhat. Adding sand helped, but you can only dump so many truckloads of sand into a garden. Compost gave life to the soil and corrected the overacid PH. You can buy compost or make your own by layering garden dirt and kitchen waste into a heap.

Perennial herbs live for years (an average of ten). If the herbs spread, as many of them tend to, the plant will live forever. Since your herbs may be in one spot for a long time, they will be healthier and happier if you feed them at least once a year. A layer of compost "dresses" the soil around the roots in fall or early spring. A spray of diluted fish emulsion or seaweed on the leaves a few times a year gives them an extra boost.

Mulch—any soft, organic material like old grass clippings or straw—can be useful in the herb garden. During the summer, a layer on the ground around the plants preserves moisture in the soil and keeps weeds down. In areas where there are winter freezes, mulch protects the roots of less hardy herbs. Mulch is not always suitable for moist areas where pests, such as slugs, snails, pill bugs, or earwigs, like to make themselves at home.

WATER

If you live in an area with regular summer rainfall, let nature do the work. Otherwise, herbs do fine watered by a drip system, by hand, or by overhead sprinklers. Avoid overhead watering during the sunniest part of the day; like most plants, herbs prefer to be watered when the sky is overcast or the sun is low in the sky.

The proper amount of water depends on where you live, but drooping leaves are your signal to grab the watering can. If leaves turn crisp on the edges or start falling off, your herbs are badly in need of water. My own garden receives almost no rain during the summer, and so I water it two times a week; more if the weather is extremely hot.

Overwatering, like overfertilizing, also creates a problem. Too much water dilutes an herb's essential oil concentration, making it less fragrant. The plants become weaker because they begin to depend upon more water and also become more susceptible to early freezing.

HUMIDITY AND SUN

You have little control over humidity unless you grow your garden in a greenhouse. In humid regions, herbs should be planted in full sun to fight mold and mildew. In addition, give your plants plenty of room and keep them well trimmed, especially along the ground.

I had great success creating a more humid environment in a lath house with an automatic watering system that sprayed a few times each day. A lath house is similar to a greenhouse, but the structure is covered with thin wooden slats (laths) instead of glass or plastic. It provides partial shade for shade-loving plants and is ideal for raising seedlings and potted plants. Not only did my plants thrive, but I enjoyed working in the refreshing dampness.

Full sun is best for your herb garden. If your only garden spot is shady, emphasize shade-loving herbs. Herbs grown in shade have less flavor, but herb gardeners can use this to their advantage. If French sorrel is too sour or watercress too bitter for your taste, then more shade will result in a more delicate flavor.

STARTING HERB PLANTS

Herb plants can be started a number of different ways. It is good to become familiar with all the propagation techniques so you can choose the most practical methods for your herb garden. You can plant seeds, sprout cuttings, or divisions from already established plants, divide plants at the roots to produce two or more plants, or encourage extra root growth to produce side shoots. It is easiest to transplant already established herb plants into your garden, but this can get expensive and the herbs you want may not be readily available.

SEEDS

Herb seeds vary in the amount of time it takes to germinate. Annuals must flower and make seed in one season, so you should expect to see them popping up in a week or two. Perennials can take two to six weeks to germinate, so be patient; they are in no hurry because they have many years ahead of them. I have disheartedly put aside flats of perennial seeds that did not come up all summer, only to have them sprout in mad profusion the next spring!

Seeds for annual herbs should be planted as early as possible in the spring. Perennials and biennials can be started in the spring or throughout the summer. Perennial seedlings that have established a good root system will usually survive the winter.

Seeds from plants originating in very cold areas need to have germination stimulated by freezing temperatures. Called stratification, this can be done by placing the seeds in water and freezing them for a couple of days in the refrigerator. Plastic ice cube trays work great because you

© Derek Fell

can use each section for a different variety of seed. If you live in an area where the ground freezes during the winter, you can sow the seeds in flats and place them outdoors to naturally freeze and thaw, so they sprout when they are ready.

Herb seeds are often very tiny. The result is that they easily shift in the soil or get washed away. I sow most herb seeds into flats so I can keep track of them. I move the flats into a warm place on chilly nights, then out into the sun the next day. My favorite flats are not the traditional cumbersome wooden boxes used by nurseries, but small plastic containers, such as the ones yogurt, cottage cheese, or tofu are packaged in. These miniflats are easy to manage and keep each seed variety separate.

One of the biggest problems new seedlings face is a fungus on the soil surface that is encouraged by dampness. Known as "damping off disease," it causes new stems to weaken and the little plants to fall over. Since the disease is carried in soil, buy sterilized potting soil from the nursery. If you want to sterilize potting soil yourself, cook dirt in the oven at 180°F (82°C) for one hour. (You had better warn your family ahead of time that you are not baking brownies!) Combine the cooked dirt with equal parts of vermiculite and sand. Use clean sand and not ocean sand, which contains salt residue. When I reuse containers for flats, I wash them, then dip them in a diluted bleach solution (20 percent bleach) to thoroughly clean them.

Fill the miniflats with about two inches of damp soil. It is best to use distilled or boiled water to avoid bacteria from well water or chlorine from treated water. Gently scatter the seeds on the surface, about twice as many as you want plants to come up, since all the seeds will not germinate. Cover the seeds with dry soil to a depth about twice as thick as one seed. Pat down gently, then use a fine spray to just dampen the surface soil. The soil should be wet, but not soaked, since too much moisture encourages fungus growth.

You can turn your miniflats into mini greenhouses by stretching plastic wrap over the top and securing it with a rubber band. The inside will remain moist as the water trapped inside keeps circulating. (Note that you do *not* need to punch holes in the container.) With this method, the seedlings probably will not need watering until they are ready for transplanting. You can even abandon them and go on vacation! An average temperature for germination is 70°F to 80°F (20°C to 25°C).

Always remove the plastic cover before the leaves touch it. Then, start watering the flat. When the second set of leaves emerge, the seedlings are ready for transplanting into the garden or into larger pots. Use a small trowel, or even a spoon, to dig out seedlings. If plants are growing tightly together, snip off extra ones at the ground instead of pulling them out and disturbing roots of other plants.

At this stage, your herbs are very tiny and vulnerable to insects, diseases, and sunstroke, and need to be "hardened off" before being exposed to the sun's full strength. They are less likely to dry out and wilt from the sun's heat in partial shade. If they go directly into the garden, cover them with upside down pots, cardboard boxes, or anything else suitable to give them a few days of protection from sun, heat, and wind. I prefer to transplant seedlings, especially slower-growing perennials, into pots or trays where they can grow sturdy before being introduced into the garden. In the early spring, most seedlings need to wait until danger of frost has passed.

CUTTINGS AND DIVISIONS

Making cuttings is the "shortcut" for starting an herb garden. First, find some herb plants, perhaps in a friend's garden. You can take cuttings from most herbs that have firm stalks, but it is often best to start off with an easy volunteer from the mint or sage family.

Cut a healthy looking stalk about four inches long. The plant should not be budding or flowering. You may be hesitant to do it, but remove all but the top four to six leaves. The herb does not have any roots to support all those leaves so this gives the roots a chance to grow enough to catch up and support more leaves.

The end of the cutting can be dipped into rooting hor-

Planter boxes allow you to plant certain herbs together. For instance, plant tea herbs in one planter and cosmetic herbs in another.

mone available at nurseries. Rooting compounds are not necessary, but can be used with difficult stem cuttings. Dip the end of the stem into water and then into the rooting compound so it coats the cut area. Another alternative is to water the cuttings with a strong willow stalk tea to encourage rooting. To make this tea, chop one cup of tree twigs and pour two quarts of hot water over them. Let sit overnight. If you've seen willows sprouting in a vase of water, you can understand how much natural rooting hormone willows contain.

Place the cuttings upright in a container of clean sand or vermiculite drenched with water. Do not use soil or liquid fertilizers. You want the cuttings to send roots out in search of nutrients. In a couple of weeks, some of the cuttings should sprout roots. Pull them out very carefully to check their progress. When they start rooting, plant them in a pot of soil and let them grow large enough to move into the garden.

ROOT DIVISION AND LAYERING

Many herbs spread by sending new roots out just under the soil's surface. The new roots sprout and can be cut away from the mother plant. You can also encourage herbs to sprout by layering. To layer a plant, first select a low-growing stem still attached to the mother plant and pile a mound of dirt over the stem. Tap the dirt down, leaving the leafy tip above ground. Eventually, the stem will root and can be left there to spread or it can be made into a division.

Old and woody herbs with inflexible lower stems can still be layered by covering the entire lower section of the herb with a dirt mound. Cut the top of the herb back to encourage new growth. Roots will sprout along the buried stems. You can also divide large plants when transplanting them.

The fastest method of starting new plants is root division. Mints and lemon grass are examples of plants that spread by sending roots out from their base to form new plants. Any section of the plant where there are stems coming out

If you are wondering where to begin, mint will reward you with rapid growth and many cups of tasty tea.

© James M. Mejuto/FPG International

of the roots is a suitable candidate for a new plant. Use a shovel to make a clean cut into the root clump to remove the new plants. Or dig up the entire plant and divide it into sections. Many herbs will easily break into new plants. Cut back the top of the new plant so it can concentrate on root growth. Pot the divisions until they are strong enough to go back into the garden. Larger sections can go directly into the garden.

Herbs whose roots grow by "crowns" make little plants around their base. Gently cut or break off the small plants from the crowns, or mother plant. If you wish, the larger roots can be transplanted back into the garden.

The focal point of this raised bed is St. Fiacre, the patron saint of gardening.

TRANSPLANTING

Any plant experiences some shock and setback when it is transplanted. Your job as an herb gardener is to make the transition as smooth as possible. Keep the roots undisturbed and away from air exposure. Have the new home ready with pots or holes already waiting. In either case, water the soil before transplanting so it is already damp.

To remove the herb plant from a pot, turn the pot upside down, holding your hand over the top, with the stems between your fingers. A few sharp taps with a trowel against the bottom of the pot will loosen the dirt, and the plant should slide out of the pot. If some soil does fall off of the roots, replace it with your free hand, then turn the plant upright and place it in its new home. Tap down the dirt around the roots and water the transplants right away in order to fill in air pockets around the roots.

It is possible to move even very large herbs around the garden. Dig straight down around the root's perimeter with a shovel. You can assume that the roots extend out at least as far as the stems. Once the circle is completed, push the shovel under the root ball and pick up the entire plant. If the root ball is large and heavy, you may need to dig under the roots to release it.

The best time to transplant into the garden is in the late afternoon or on overcast days. Cover the new transplants with inverted pots for a few days until they are well established. Garden pots work well since they have a vent hole in the top. Water clay pots to keep them extra cool during hot days. Large herbs that have just been transplanted can be covered with cardboard boxes or wet burlap bags supported on three sticks lashed together at the top into a "tepee." Your herbs will appreciate this transition time to become adjusted to their new home.

Trim back the foliage on large herbs just before transplanting to avoid "transplant shock." Have tools and water handy, and bring a basket to collect the trimmings.

© Anita Sabarese

Garden design can be based not only on contrasts in color, but in subtle varieties in texture, as seen in the grays of lamb's ears and artemisia.

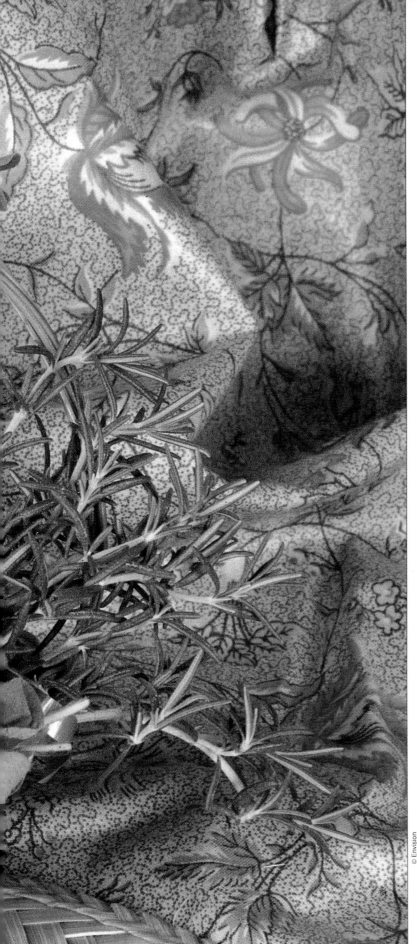

CHAPTER THREE

HARVESTING HERBS

One of the greatest rewards the herb garden offers is a bountiful harvest. A typical summer morning finds me with basket in hand, a straw hat shading early morning rays from my eyes, strolling through my herb garden clipping and snipping. Soon my basket is filled with sprigs that will flavor food, scent potpourri, and fill my house with color for the next year.

Your garden will provide you with the best-quality herbs possible, as you grow, harvest, and dry them with care. Even average-quality herbs harvested from your own garden will be better than those from the store. You can enjoy and judge the quality of your herbs by how they look, smell, and taste.

Perennial herbs grown in beds should be harvested so that the plant retains its shape, and so there is ample foliage left to support the plant for years to come. Annuals can be harvested solely by frequently picking off the tops. This encourages the plants to grow bushier and send out side branches.

WHEN TO HARVEST HERBS

A few general guidelines are all that you need to produce garden herbs with the best flavor, fragrance, and color. Ideally, each herb should be harvested at its peak potency. The time of year and the time of day are the most important considerations.

© Derek Fell

TIME OF DAY

Old herb books say to harvest herbs in the morning, just after the dew dries from the leaves, and for good reason. Plants concentrate their essential oils during the night, then release them as the sun begins to warm the morning. Walk through an herb garden on a hot day and notice that the air around you is filled with delicious herbal scents as these oils are released.

Whenever possible, harvest the garden when it has not been watered or rained on for a few days. Since the object is to dry the plants, the less water they contain when picked, the better. The exception would be a dusty environment. In this case, give the plants a light sprinkle to wash them off the day before harvesting.

TIME OF YEAR

The best-quality herbs are harvested at their prime. There is no need for complicated charts and graphs to know when to pick each herb. Simply watch your garden grow. Plants change throughout the year as they respond to the seasons. In spring, warmer, longer days literally pull plants from their roots in bursts of energy. Leaves reach maximum potency just before the first flowers open. Most herbs will resume growth after they are cut back and can be harvested two to four times in the summer and into the fall.

Once they begin blooming, plants concentrate on their flowers. Lower leaves begin turning brown and lose potency. Most flowers should be harvested just before they are fully open; a few, however, are picked while still in their bud stage. Don't be shy about picking them—it encourages more blooms. Seeds are formed after the flowers die back. Harvest these just as they ripen, but before they fall from the plant.

Dig roots during the plant's winter dormant cycle, when they are most potent. During the cold months, roots serve as a storage system. Many references suggest harvesting roots only in the fall or early spring, but if the ground does not freeze where you live, roots can be gathered throughout the winter. Biennial roots, which live only two years, need to be harvested in their first fall or second spring. By the second fall, the plant is ready to die and the root loses potency. You might want to stake out their location in the fall so you can find them after they die down. By the way, useful roots are almost always perennials or biennials since the roots of annuals are not needed for winter storage.

It may not always be possible to harvest your herbs at the optimum time of their cycle or hour of day. If you miss their peak, you can still harvest them. Judge an herb's quality by smelling and tasting it. If the flavor and taste are strong, they are good. When culinary herbs like oregano and basil have already gone to flower, harvest the topmost leaves and the flowers, too. Most flowers carry the same scent and flavor as the leaves.

© Frances Stein

Most herbs, including oregano, should be harvested before they bloom.

HOW TO HARVEST

A sharp knife, pruning clippers, or scissors will make clean cuts on the stems for harvesting leaves or flowers. Avoid tearing the stem or making jagged cuts. You will find that many flowers and some leaves are easier to pick by hand. When harvesting, be sure to leave a substantial part for the plant's health. Either cut a few stems back all the way or cut many stems halfway down. Cut plants with hard stems, such as rosemary, back to last year's growth; if you want to shape the bush, then prune it back even farther.

When I first began herb gardening, it always seemed that herbs such as dill dropped their seeds the day before I was ready to harvest them. I finally learned to beat them to it! Wait until the seeds begin to come off easily into your hand. Place a paper bag, upside down, over the top of the plant and tie the top of the bag tightly around the stem. Any seeds that haven't already fallen off will fall into the bag. When it is time to harvest, cut off the stem and turn the "plant bag" upside down and hang it up until the seeds are completely dry. By then, most seeds will have fallen off, but if any still remain on the stem, gently brush them off into the bag.

Dig roots with the shovel pointing straight down to avoid slicing them. Or, if the soil is loose enough, pull them up with a garden fork. Once you have uncovered the root and knocked off any loose dirt, give it a short soak in

Fresh mint and rosemary join ginger root en route to a feast.

cold water to rinse off any remaining dirt. (Hot water or long soaks can leach out the root's properties.) Scrub the root right away, before dirt becomes permanently embedded in crevices and pockets on its surface.

Keep herbs out of direct sun after harvesting them. The sun will blacken them and quickly evaporate their essential oils. There is nothing so discouraging for gardeners as putting all their love, care, and work into their herb gardens and then have their beautiful harvest turn to compost.

DRYING HERBS

Country gardeners used to dry their herbs by tying them into bunches and hanging them from attic rafters. All summer and fall, the attic in my old house was filled with picturesque drying herbs. It was very warm and dark and the side windows provided air circulation. You may not have the perfect herb-drying attic, but any dark, warm place will do.

Notice how quickly clothes dry on hot, breezy days. The same is true for herbs. It is fine if the drying area cools at night, though the drying time will be extended. Herb growers living in humid climates use forced air dryers to circulate hot air around the herbs. Total darkness is not necessary, but keep drying herbs away from direct sunlight to retain their color and essential oils.

Choose a drying method that is most practical for your space and for the herb's eventual purpose. The advantage of hanging herbs upside down is that they dry with straight stems and upright flowers then can be used in dried flower arrangements. To make bunches, cut the stems long enough to tie with string or rubber bands. The size of the bunches depends on the air's humidity. In my dry climate, I tie nice, big herb bundles with about fifteen stems to a bunch. On the other hand, if you live in a more humid climate, tie only a few stems together to prevent mold. When in doubt, keep an eye out for mold growing where the stems are tightly tied together.

There are many ingenious drying racks for hanging herbs. A folding clothes-drying rack, the kind made with

© Tony Cenicola

long dowels, holds about fifty bunches. It is portable, can be set up almost anywhere, and folds for easy storage. Another type of clothes dryer suitable for herbs is the wooden wall racks that lie flat against the wall, then fan out for hanging. A hanging umbrella-style clothes rack will also work for a few herbs. Your kitchen walls can be decorated with bunches of herbs that are light enough to hang from push pins. Wooden wall racks with pegs, such as Shaker-styled hat racks, can also accommodate drying herbs.

A paper bag makes a handy, portable dryer that keeps sun and dust off the herbs. Put a bunch into the bag with the stems protruding from the top. Tie a string tightly around the top of the bag and stems. In humid areas, cut little "U"-shaped windows in the bag to increase air flow. This is a great method if you harvest in the countryside. Hang the bags anywhere, even outside in the shade. Yes, your neighbors will probably ask you if this is some new way to keep crows out of the trees, but you can't beat the method for ease and practicality.

Herbs can also be dried by laying them on screens. This is especially useful for flowers or herbs too small to tie in bundles. A well-washed window screen will work, or you can custom-make your own by stretching stainless steel screening (from a hardware store) over a wooden frame. Individual flowers can be carefully pushed through the holes in a large mesh screen. Screens can be stacked about eight inches apart using bricks or wood-block supports or you can construct a wooden frame they slide into. When I was drying herbs commercially, I set six-by-four-foot screens into tall frames that held eight screens each. For smaller jobs, eighteen-inch frames are a good size. Small screens can also be suspended in tiers from string and hung in warm areas of the house.

When you lay out the herbs on screens, layer them thinly so air can circulate freely around them. Stiff herbs will provide enough air space around them, but limp herbs need to be stirred or tossed every day to dry them evenly and prevent molding. In humid areas, you may have to lay the herbs so there is no overlap.

STORING HERBS

You will know when your herbs are dry when they are crispy and break easily. Unless you want to keep the leaves on the stem, remove them by gently running your hand from the top down. Leaves tend to grow upward at an angle, so a downward motion pulls them off quickly.

Herbs are best stored in airtight jars or plastic bags, away from light, heat, and moisture. Personally, I find culinary herbs so attractive I can not resist putting some in clear spice jars out in the kitchen. I do keep most herbs in a dark cupboard and keep refilling my small, clear jars

from these larger storage jars. Herbs stored in jars tend to stay a little fresher then those kept in plastic bags.

Label herbs when you first put them in containers so you will be sure to know what they are and when they were harvested. If any droplets collect on the inside of the container, act fast to rescue the herbs. Such moisture tells you they were not completely dry and are destined to mold unless you take them out and finish drying them.

It is often said the flowers keep for a year and roots and bark keep for two years, but there is no exact cutoff date. The better they are stored the longer they will last. Store

© Derek Fell

your herbs whole or cut instead of ground if you are keeping them for longer than a couple of months. Ground herbs quickly lose their essential oils, flavor, and scent. Judge the quality of dried herbs the same way you determine the quality of fresh ones. If they look and smell the way they did when you first dried them, the herbs are still good.

I have little trouble with bugs infesting my dried herbs. Many herbs, such as santolina and wormwood, are bug repellents. Roots are the most susceptible to bug invasion. The ones to watch out for are brown mealy moths and grain weevils (the same bugs that eat grains in the kitchen). If you discover webs, little holes in the herbs, or if you find the bugs themselves, you have an infestation. If the herbs are salvageable, placing them in a freezer for two days kills the bugs.

DRYING TECHNIQUES

Special drying techniques preserve flowers or other delicate plants for dried floral and herbal arrangements. These techniques are more work, but are great for herbs that are difficult to dry by simply hanging bunches or laying them on screens. Reserve these techniques for delicate flowers like rosebuds, lilacs, or other plants that tend to shrivel or lose their color when air-dried. Sturdy herbs like yarrow, tansy, marjoram, and oregano do not need these special techniques.

DESICCANTS

Materials called desiccants absorb water from plants quickly, so that when they dry they retain most of their original shape and color. One old-fashioned method used ground flour. I find medium-ground cornmeal works best. A less-favored method, popular in the seventeenth century, uses sand; however, sand is less absorbent and too heavy for delicate flowers. Hobby stores sell a modern version called silica gel, which is known to chemists as a xerogel of silicic acid. It has increased absorbency (40 percent of its own weight) and a quicker drying time.

Put about one-half inch of either cornmeal or silica gel in a plastic box, which prevents moisture from being drawn in from the surrounding air. A cardboard box will work if it is kept in a dry place. Lay the flowers or other plant material on top of the absorbent material and carefully sprinkle more material in and around them until they are completely covered. Make sure the material has contact with all the petals. Be careful not to bend the plants when covering them, unless you want a special effect.

The flowers take about two weeks to dry with cornmeal and one week with silica gel. When dry, they should feel like paper and have no flexibility left. They are very delicate and break easily at this stage. If left too long, the flowers become too brittle and fall apart. Flowers removed too soon can droop or loose color. Scoop or pour out the silica gel or cornmeal, then carefully lift the plants out with a fork. Remove the flowers, then carefully brush off excess material will a soft watercolor or makeup brush.

Both cornmeal and silica gel are reusable. Most types of silica gel contain blue crystals that turn pink when they have reached maximum absorbency. To dry these crystals for reuse, place them in an oven set at 300°F (148°C). Store either material in an airtight container so it won't absorb moisture.

MICROWAVE DRYING

Using a microwave is the newest and fastest way to dry herbs and flowers that will be used for herbal wreaths and other crafts projects. Plants can be microwaved by placing them between two paper plates. A microwave oven will also shorten the time it takes to dry plants in silica gel (as described above). Dry the plants buried in silica gel in a microwave oven container without a lid or in a cardboard box.

The cooking and setting times vary with different types of microwave ovens and the number and type of plants, so some experimentation is needed. It takes about two minutes to dry plants buried in one-half pound of silica gel. The setting is low, between 200 and 350 watts. Afterwards, the flowers will need about 10 to 30 minutes of standing time before removing them from the silica gel.

Not all plants dry well in a microwave oven. Very delicate plants, those that lose their color easily, and ones with thick leaves or petals, often look better dried in silica gel or cornmeal.

GLYCERINE

Herbs and flowers for wreath making and other decorative purposes can be preserved with glycerine, a nontoxic by-product of soap making. The preserved plants stay flexible, which is important if you are making head wreaths, flowered hats, or any dried flower craft that may occasionally be touched or bumped.

Not all flowers lend themselves to glycerine preservation but those that do provide herbal crafts with more variety. The colorful flowers of annual statice are most commonly preserved with glycerine, since they are very brittle when air-dried. It is fun to experiment with different types of flowers and leaves to see what effect glycerine gives them. Glycerine does darken colors, although the slight darkening is often attractive, giving floral crafts a nice accent. For example, white flowers turn ivory and many leaves become dark and leathery.

Glycerine is sold in drug stores and some craft shops. Stir one part glycerine into two parts warm water. Set the flowers you wish to preserve in at least four inches of the mixture in a jar or vase. The plants must be freshly cut to be able to absorb the glycerine and water mix. Pick them from your herb and flower garden, or buy them at a flower or farmer's market.

It takes about two weeks to treat the flowers. If they drink up all of the mixture, add more. When they are done, they will be flexible and soft to the touch, even though they are no longer fresh. If left in the glycerine solution too long, they become sticky. The lower stem that was in the glycerine solution will be too sticky to work with, so cut it off. Store the plants in cardboard boxes in a dry place until you are ready to use them.

© Tony Cenicola

CHAPTER FOUR

HERBS IN THE COUNTRY KITCHEN

A well-known expression calls something exciting the spice of life. The word *spice* also describes the zesty effect some herbs have on foods. Herbs play many roles in making meals a memorable experience. Since oils, vinegars, mustards, and spice combinations are so often incorporated into cooking, herbs offer a quick and easy way to spice up your life. In this chapter I am going to describe some of their many uses.

Herbs can turn an ordinary bottle of vinegar into a gourmet delight. The most popular herbal vinegars are sage, rosemary, thyme, tarragon, and basil. But do not stop there. Put your imagination in gear to create all kinds of vinegars. Try parsley, oregano, or peppermint, for example. Those who like a little bite can even mince fresh onions or garlic and leave them in the vinegar.

Your herb garden is filled with many herbs just waiting for experimentation. Some of the most unique varieties can be found only in your garden. Chive flowers make an excellent vinegar. Far more interesting than the chives themselves, the flowers turn the vinegar a lovely purple and add a definite chive flavor. Another unusual but tasty vinegar is made from salad burnet. As its name implies, it was once a popular salad herb, but its strong flavor makes it best suited for herbal vinegar.

If you do not have an herb garden, some grocery stores sell fresh herbs, or you can buy them at a farmer's market. Fresh herbs give vinegar the best flavor, but in a pinch, dried herbs will work.

Any type of vinegar can be used. White vinegar brings out herbal colors, such as the purple hues of chive flowers or purple basil. Apple cider vinegar is sometimes preferred for its full taste and health properties. Parsley turns cider vinegar an attractive pale shade. Wine vinegar imparts a gourmet touch. Other possibilities include barley and rice vinegars.

HERBAL VINEGARS

1 cup fresh herbs, chopped (your choice)

1 pint vinegar

a widemouthed jar

Coarsely chop the herbs you select. Put 1 cup of the chopped herbs in a clean, widemouthed jar. Fill the jar loosely without packing the herbs down. Add one pint of vinegar, making sure all the herbs are completely covered. Stir to release any trapped air bubbles and put a tight lid on the jar. After about two weeks at room temperature, the vinegar will have extracted the herb's flavor. By then it should taste and smell delicious! Strain the herbs out of the vinegar.

This vinegar will be full flavored. If you prefer it milder, add 1 to 2 cups of plain vinegar. I make concentrated vinegars because it takes less room to process and store all the different varieties my garden produces. I can always dilute them if needed.

Pour your herbal vinegar into a fancy glass bottle that shows off the color. The final touch is to add a sprig of the dried or fresh herb. Poke it into the bottle so it is suspended instead of floating on the top. The herbs you see in gourmet herbal vinegars are decorations added after the vinegar is made. That one sprig is not enough to flavor an entire bottle of vinegar.

© Rogers Assoc.

© Steven Mark Needham/Envision

HERBAL OILS

While herbal vinegars are popular gourmet items, you rarely see herbal oils. It is too bad, since the oils can add another dimension to cooking. The technique is similar to herbal vinegars, but the herbs are covered with oil instead of vinegar. Any vegetable oil will work, although virgin olive and other strong tasting oils overpower mild flavored herbs. It is best to store any oil, herbal or otherwise, in a cool place.

1 cup fresh herbs, chopped (your choice)

1 pint vegetable oil

a widemouthed jar

Chop 1 cup fresh or dried herbs and cover them with 1 pint of oil, making sure all herbs are submerged. Stir to release any air bubbles. Put the oil in a warm place (an upper kitchen cabinet will do) for three days. The location does not need constant warmth. Strain out the herbs, and the oil is ready. (If for some reason you do not strain the oil right away, there is no hurry.) This oil can be made into salad dressing or used in any recipe calling for oil. A standard dressing recipe combines two parts oil with one part vinegar (herbal, of course).

Variations: Herbal blends offer many possibilities. These can be processed all in one bottle, but it is more fun to make separate vinegars and have a whole selection from which to choose. If you would like to make ethnic herbal oils, use appropriate oils as your base. Ethnic specialties also owe much of their individuality to particular herbs. Herbs traditionally associated with a certain culture can be used to develop herbal blends. Here are a few ideas to spark your imagination.

Italian Oil: Olive oil with basil, oregano, and marjoram
Greek Oil: Olive oil with thyme, rosemary, and bay leaves
East Indian Oil: Sesame oil with coriander, cumin, and cayenne (optional)
Chinese Oil: Peanut oil with black pepper and ginger (use half quantities)
European Oil: Safflower oil with tarragon, sage, and parsley
Mexican Oil: Sunflower with cumin, coriander, chili peppers, and dried tomatoes.

Herbal oils can also be made by leaving the herbs in the jar instead of being strained out. Use whole or chopped fresh herbs. (If you use dried herbs, be sure to remove hard parts of the leaves and even small stems, since these will only be slightly softened by the oil.) Cover with oil, stirring to remove any air bubbles. Let sit at room temperature for one week, then refrigerate.

HONEYED GINGER

Honeyed ginger is one of my favorites. The honey sweetens ginger's sharp bite and it takes on a spicy, gingery flavor. The ginger pieces can be eaten like candy and the honey used to make special treats or used by itself.

½ cup fresh ginger, chopped

1 cup honey

a jar

Cut thin slices of fresh ginger. Fill a very clean jar (scrub the jar well and pour boiling water into it a few times) with a few inches of the slices. Heat the honey to liquefy it and pour it over the ginger slices. Stir with a knife or chopstick to eliminate all the air bubbles between the pieces. Add a few more inches of ginger and pour more honey over them, again pushing out any air bubbles. When you are done, the honey should completely cover the ginger.

The honey will become more liquefied as it absorbs moisture from the ginger. After about three weeks, the ginger is ready for eating, but if properly stored, it will last for years. Keep it in a cool place to prevent the liquefied honey from turning into mead (a fermented honey drink). If it does eventually bubble a little, slightly open the lid to let the bubbles escape.

Variation: You can make other types of honeyed herbs. The Chinese preserve many fresh foods in honey. Honeyed garlic, a combination of the pungent and the sweet, is one of their specialties. To make this condiment, peel whole garlic cloves and cover them completely with warm honey. Let the mixture sit a few weeks, then enjoy. Another idea is to stir 1 tablespoon of ground herbs, such as cinnamon, into honey. Let sit for at least two weeks. The honey will soften the fine herb pieces and the whole concoction can be spread on toast or used in any dish calling for honey.

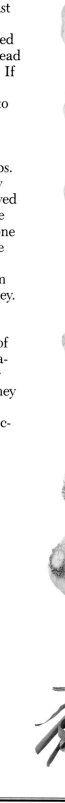

HERBAL MUSTARD

2 tablespoons ground mustard

2 tablespoons flour

½ teaspoon each
    turmeric
    ginger

1 cup apple cider vinegar

½ cup water

1 tablespoon honey (optional)

a jar

Mix mustard, flour, and spices together. Mix vinegar, warm water, and honey together. Combine dry and wet ingredients in a saucepan. Bring mixture to a boil, turn down the heat, and let simmer for two minutes. Pack into very clean jars while warm. Push out any air pockets. Store in a cool place.

This mustard will last for many months, although its flavor does change as it ages. Mustard connoisseurs say it is best when not more than a few weeks old. One way to keep it fresh is to add a slice of fresh lemon to the jar, on top of the mustard. Replace the lemon with a fresh slice every few days.

Variations: The consistency may be thinned with more water or thickened with more flour, but watch out. Water will make the mustard hotter. In fact, for a very hot mustard, replace ¼ cup vinegar with water (vinegar counteracts the "heat"). If you prefer a mellow version, use oil or mayonnaise instead of water.

To give mustard a French flair, use red wine vinegar, or even wine instead of vinegar. The true French Dijon mustard replaces vinegar with champagne! Duplicate Chinese mustard by using flat beer instead of vinegar.

Different herbs added to mustard create distinct flavors. Make an extra-hot mustard by adding ½ teaspoon of grated horseradish. Horseradish's flavor is produced while you grate it, so add it fresh, if possible. One teaspoon of whole mustard seeds provides an interesting texture. Whole black mustard seeds give mustard color contrast. A dash (⅛ teaspoon) of powdered cloves or dill or both is often added to mustard. A teaspoon of any herb or spice blend from this chapter creates even more mustard varieties.

PICKLED HERBS

Pickled herbs provide a tasty highlight to meals. They can be served as a side dish or incorporated into other foods. Use them to spice up stir-fried food, soups, and stews.

Herbs that are especially appropriate for pickles include chopped basil, French sorrel, chive leaves, whole nasturtium flowers or pods, and whole, peeled garlic cloves. Pickling makes a lot of wild herbs, such as wild sorrel, young dock, and dandelion leaves (ones most people would never invite to their dinner table), quite palatable. If you have a flair for the unusual, give one of these a try. They are sure to be a showstopper at your next dinner party!

1 cup fresh herbs, whole

1 pint vinegar, your choice

1 tablespoon spices, ground (optional)

a jar

I like to use old canning jars to show off the pickled herbs on my shelf, but any jar or crock will do. Take herb leaves off their stems and place in a clean jar. Completely cover the herbs with vinegar, stirring to make sure there are no air bubbles. For a variation, add pickling spices or another herb blend to the vinegar to give it added flavor. Let sit for at least four weeks. Store them in a cool place, but as long as the herbs remain submerged, there is no need to refrigerate.

Variations: Mint Sauce: Pickled mint leaves, either chopped or whole, can easily be made into mint sauce by mixing 2 tablespoons of warmed honey with ½ cup of mint vinegar.

Pickled Nettles: An interesting condiment combining vinegar and oil in the same preparation. Fresh stinging nettles, for example, make a very different, yet delicious, pickle. I learned this one from an Oregon herbalist, Svevo Brooks. Cook them first to remove the stingers, then prepare the whole leaves in either a vinegar or an oil according to the instructions above. When they are ready, drain off extra liquid and submerge the pickled nettles in olive oil, or the oil nettles in vinegar. If you wish, add a few cloves of whole garlic or sprigs of dill to enhance the flavor.

HERB SALT AND SEASONINGS

There is often not enough time to do the selecting, grinding, and preparation involved in making herbal blends from fresh herbs, especially if you are preparing a meal at the last minute. One alternative is to make herb salts and spice blends ahead of time. Most standard recipes can be adapted by replacing the total amount of all herbs required with your spice blend. Spice blends can season soups, stews, breads, muffins, bread sticks, eggs, beans, pasta, potatoes, cakes, pies, cookies, and specialty dishes. The following recipes offer an assortment of flavors to brighten any table.

If you make a number of blends, you can choose whether tonight's meal will be Italian, Oriental, or Mexican—all with just a few shakes of the spice jar. It may be common to match spices with the appropriate food, but why not be daring? Why not try some Chinese refried beans, an Italian stir fry, or Mexican pizza for a change of pace?

Start with good-quality dried herbs from your garden or buy whole or cut herbs. Avoid purchasing ground herbs since they will have lost much of their flavor. Grind the herbs in a coffee grinder, blender, flour mill, with a mortar and pestle, or whatever is convenient in your kitchen. If pieces of stems remain in the blend, strain them out with a colander, kitchen strainer, or flour sifter. The herbs can be finely ground or left a little chunky, depending on your preference. Small chunks of herbs give a variety in texture to a ground mixture. The following recipes all call for ground herbs, unless otherwise indicated.

© Burke/Triolo

© Robert Lima/Envision

HERBAL SALT SUBSTITUTE

1 tablespoon each, ground
  basil
  coriander
  thyme

2 teaspoons each, ground
  cumin
  onion
  parsley

1 teaspoon each, ground
  garlic (minced)
  mustard
  paprika
  cayenne (optional)
  kelp (optional)

This all-around handy blend gives herbal zest to any meal. Put it on the table in a salt shaker and use it as a salt replacement.

ITALIAN SPICE

1 tablespoon basil, ground

2 teaspoons marjoram, ground

1 teaspoon oregano, ground

½ teaspoon each, minced
  garlic
  onion

These herbs are famous for what they do for pizza, spaghetti, and almost any tomato dish. If you are a garlic or an onion fan, you can double those quantities, but be careful not to overpower the basil. Its sweet taste is part of the secret of Italian cooking.

MIDDLE EASTERN SPICE

1 tablespoon cumin

2 teaspoons parsley

1 teaspoon each
  black pepper
  garlic
  onion

This spice blend flavors beans or any other dish you think is worthy of an exotic Middle Eastern flavor.

The spicy dishes of Mexico, India, Thailand, and China all use mustard and peppers with a liberal hand.

MEXICAN CHILI SPICE

1 tablespoon paprika

2 teaspoons each
cinnamon
coriander
oregano

1 teaspoon each
black pepper
cayenne (or other chili
pepper)
garlic
mustard seed, yellow

There are many types of chili peppers, each with a slightly different taste and pungency. This recipe makes a hot chili, so if your taste buds prefer life a bit more mellow, use ½ teaspoon instead of 1 teaspoon of the last four ingredients. For a sweeter chili, double the cinnamon. Kidney beans are the most common to put in chili, but try it out on other types of legumes, like lentils and peas.

EAST INDIAN SPICE

1 tablespoon each, ground
coriander
cumin
turmeric

1 teaspoon each
allspice
black mustard seed, whole
cayenne
cinnamon

Black or white peppers, chili peppers, garlic, and yellow or black mustard heat up a curry. If cooling down is more your style, use paprika instead of cayenne. You might have an herb called curry plant in your garden. Although it is not an ingredient in East Indian cooking, its smell and taste resemble curry, thus giving it its name. When curry became the rage, but spices from the East were too expensive for most Europeans to afford, they substituted this native plant.

THAI SPICE

*1 tablespoon lemon grass
    leaves (can be fresh,
    chopped instead of dried)*

*1 teaspoon each
    black pepper
    coriander (or fresh
        cilantro, if available)
    ginger*

Thai food is gaining in popularity. Noted for its hot and sweet combination, it often contains lemon grass, an herb used more commonly for tea than as a flavoring.

Spice Blend Variations: Have fun coming up with your own ideas for other spice blends. If you want a salty taste, but are trying to cut down on your salt intake, add a small amount of kelp powder, available in the herb section of health food stores.

Chopped, dehydrated vegetables give your spice blend a new taste and look. Tomatoes and red or green peppers make it especially colorful in clear spice bottles. Dry your own vegetables in a dehydrator or buy them already dried at health food or grocery stores.

© Steven Mark Needham/Envision

Ground coriander gives a distinctly different taste than either coriander seeds or cilantro leaves.

© Derek Fell

FRENCH LOUISIANA SPICE

1 tablespoon allspice

2 teaspoons thyme

1 teaspoon each
bay
black pepper

½ teaspoon each
cayenne
cloves

This traditional cuisine combines herbs from many cultures. Cayenne and bay from the New World blend with spices of the Far East. Turn this recipe into a gumbo by adding 2 teaspoons ground sassafras leaves to thicken and flavor the dish.

CHINESE FIVE-SPICE

1 tablespoon each
cinnamon
fennel

1 teaspoon each
star anise
black pepper
cloves

All of these herbs are easily obtained, except for star anise, which is sold in the Oriental food section. If you can not find it, regular anise has a very similar taste. While looking for Oriental foods, buy Szechuan pepper instead of regular black pepper, if you can.

GIFT IDEAS

All of the items in this chapter make wonderful, thoughtful gifts anyone will enjoy! Gifts to dress up the culinary arts are appreciated throughout the year as housewarming or birthday gifts and are especially thoughtful for those friends who seem to have everything! Even people who do little cooking can use an herbal vinegar or a jar of flavorful mustard.

Combine a number of culinary treats in a bread or fruit basket and instantly you have an edible gift basket. How about an herbal vinegar and oil set with some spicy mustard, a spice blend or two, and a pot holder? Decorate the basket with a sprig of dried herbs and a bow and your gift is complete.

HERBAL DINING, COUNTRY STYLE

Country dining is known for its simplicity, yet it is also famous for its fine taste. Every gourmet cook knows that herbs have the ability to turn a good meal into a delicious feast. The finest cooks prefer using fresh herbs, such as the ones you can harvest from your own herb garden.

Country dining encompasses everything from a picnic to a clambake to a seven-course Thanksgiving or Christmas dinner, and everything from jams and preserves to cider and apple pie.

Fresh and dried herbs can be the stars of any country meal, and the recipes included here are sure to please every family member and friend.

*All recipes serve four, unless otherwise noted.

Sorrel soup is a traditional French dish that will suit either a country table or a formal banquet.

© Burke/Triolo

FRENCH SORREL SOUP

French sorrel is easily grown in your herb garden. Its pleasingly sour, lemony flavor gives this soup a delicious tang.

2 cups French sorrel leaves, chopped

1 tablespoon vegetable oil or butter

4 cups water

¼ cup milk

¼ cup cream

1 bouquet garni (see below)

chervil and parsley, chopped

Sauté leaves in oil or butter. Stir in water, milk, cream, and bouquet garni, and bring to a simmer. Turn off heat and let sit ten minutes. Garnish with chervil and parsley (or fines herbes) and serve.

Variations: You can make a mild version with chard or, if you are adventuresome, make a "wild" soup with any edible wild green, including chicory, dock, and wild sorrel. (Just be sure it is properly identified!) While in Greece, I enjoyed a similar dish called *horta* (or "plant"), which was prepared with fresh, young dandelion leaves.

© Burke/Triolo

BOUQUET GARNI

These small bouquets are used to garnish (*garni*) soups and stew. For the best flavor, use fresh herbs whenever possible. Both bouquet garni and fines herbes are French seasonings that vary depending on the cook's preferences and what is handy in the garden at the time.

4 sprigs parsley

2 sprigs thyme

1 bay leaf

1 sprig chervil

1 sprig marjoram

Tie the herbs' stems into a bundle with string. Add one bouquet for every 2 quarts of soup about twenty minutes before the soup is done. Before serving, pull out the bouquet and discard.

Variations: A dried bouquet garni can be made with chopped herbs tied in four-inch squares of cheesecloth. Store them for future use in a tightly covered container.

FINES HERBES

Fines Herbes is a blend of fresh herbs used in sauces and cheese and egg dishes. In a pinch, you can replace them with dried herbs, prepared the same way as a bouquet garni. To retain their fresh flavor, they are added to a dish just before serving.

1 sprig each
parsley
tarragon
chervil
chives

Finely mince herbs, add to dish, and serve.

CREAM SAUCES

Even though cream sauces are easy to make, they have a way of giving any dish a gourmet touch. A basic cream sauce has dozens of variations, depending on the herbs you choose.

BASIC CREAM SAUCE

2 tablespoons oil or butter

2 tablespoons flour

1½ cups milk

1 bouquet garni

Place ingredients in a pan over very low heat. Stir for three to five minutes to thicken. (For a thicker sauce, cook in 350°F oven for twenty minutes.) Remove the bouquet garni. Pour on vegetables, grain, or potato dishes to supplement a main course or use as a soup base.

Variations: Prepare the Basic Cream Sauce, then add the following:
Sauce Blanche: ¼ cup mushrooms, very finely chopped. Finish by stirring in ⅛ teaspoon nutmeg
Aurore Sauce: ¼ cup tomato sauce

Soubise Sauce: ½ cup onions, chopped and sautéed in 1 tablespoon oil
Ravigote Sauce: Two shallots cooked for a couple minutes in 2 tablespoons vinegar and 1 teaspoon prepared mustard.* Top with a sprinkle of freshly ground pepper and nutmeg
Sharp Sauce: Add pickled nasturtium pods*
Curry Sauce: Add 1 teaspoon curry powder*
Herb Sauce: Add 2 tablespoons of any herbal seasonings*
Mustard Sauce: Add 1 teaspoon mustard*
Allemande Sauce: Add ½ cup soup stock, 2 tablespoons cream, and 1 tablespoon lemon juice
Poulette Sauce: Garnish allemande sauce with finely chopped parsley

*See Chapter Four

© Brian Leatart

Cream sauce can easily be converted into a soup by adding an equal amount of water to other liquid ingredients called for in a recipe.

PESTO

Pesto is a popular condiment that goes with many dishes. It is delicious with pasta, potatoes, bread, or muffins. Pesto is an excellent way to keep herbs fresh for months after they are harvested. I like to freeze it in ice-cube trays, then store the cubes in a plastic bag in the freezer to keep them handy throughout the year.

⅛ cup pine nuts

¼ cup olive oil

1 cup fresh basil

Parmesan cheese, grated (optional)

Chop the nuts in the blender. Blend in olive oil, basil, garlic, and cheese. To store, press into a container and freeze, or cover with a thin layer of olive oil and keep refrigerated.

Variations: Pesto is usually made from fresh basil, but don't limit yourself, especially if you have a garden full of herbs. Other fresh soft-leaved herbs like parsley can replace the basil or be combined with it. Pine nuts can be replaced by walnuts, or for some really unique flavors, try cashews or pistachios! Traditional it is not, but it makes a new and exciting herbal condiment. For yet another variation, add 1 teaspoon of one of Chapter Four's herbal seasonings.

© Burke/Triolo

HERB MUFFINS

Muffins from my kitchen are never boring because of the selection of herbs from which I can choose. It doesn't take much time to make muffins from scratch, but you can also add herbs to a plain muffin mix.

2 cups flour

2 tablespoons baking powder

½ teaspoon salt

2 eggs

2 tablespoons vegetable oil

¼ cup honey

1 cup milk

2 tablespoons herbs (your choice)

Sift flour, baking powder, and salt together. Beat eggs, add oil, honey, and milk.

Combine dry and liquid ingredients and mix. Preheat oven to 400°F. Pour dough into a well-oiled muffin tin and bake for twenty-five minutes, or until done. Remove from the oven and let cool a few minutes before popping muffins from the pan. This makes about one dozen muffins. Try a warm, spicy muffin with herbal honey, herb butter, or pesto.

Variations: Suggestions for seasonings to include: allspice, anise, basil, cinnamon, cloves, ginger, orange peel, sage, or thyme, or an herbal blend from Chapter Four. You can even make different-flavored muffins in the same batch. Mix the ingredients, without the spice, so the batter is still slightly lumpy. Pour a few muffins' worth of batter into an extra bowl. Add about ¼ teaspoon herb per muffin, finish stirring, and pour into the muffin pan. Pour a little more batter into the extra bowl, add another herb, and continue until you have a selection of flavored muffins.

HERBAL SPREADS

Herbal spreads and dips dress up muffins, breads, and crackers. For the following recipes, use a single herb or choose an herbal seasoning from Chapter Four.

Always keep fresh parsley on hand to be blended into a cheese spread or to serve as a garnish.

HERBAL CHEESE SPREAD

1 cup cottage cheese

3 tablespoons milk

1 tablespoon herbal seasoning

1 teaspoon chives or parsley, chopped

Whip cottage cheese, milk, and seasoning together in a blender until smooth. Garnish with chopped herbs.

Variation: Replace the cottage cheese with cream cheese.

HERBAL BUTTER

½ cup butter (one stick)

2 teaspoons herbal seasoning

Let butter sit out until softened. Mix in herbs. Shape by placing in a container or heat it just enough to pour into butter or candy molds. Return butter to refrigerator to harden before serving.

Variations: Use margarine or other butter substitute. For garlic butter, add two grated cloves of finely minced fresh garlic.

© Steven Mark Needham/Envision

COUNTRY TEA BLENDS

Herbal teas are a healthy alternative to black tea or coffee. Create your own blends by mixing equal parts of your tastiest garden herbs, or buy bulk herbs from a natural food store. If one flavor predominates, reduce the amount until you get the recipe just right. Teas can be made from fresh or dried herbs. Use 1 teaspoon per cup either way. Fewer fresh herbs fit into a teaspoon, but they are stronger tasting.

Steep flowers and leaves in a teapot or cup by covering with boiling water and letting sit for five minutes. Ground herbs in tea bags steep even faster, taking only two or three minutes. Roots and barks take longer to extract, so heat at a very low simmer for five to ten minutes. Keep a lid on the teapot or pan to keep in the flavor. Strain the herbs, add sweetener if you like, and enjoy the tea! In any season you can keep a jar of prepared tea in the refrigerator for a couple of days, handy whenever you want it.

After working in your herb garden on a hot summer day, enjoy a glass of iced herbal tea. Prepare a tea, let it cool, then add ice cubes. Jazz up iced tea with carbonation by making a concentrated tea, using 2 teaspoons of herb per cup instead of 1. When the tea cools, add an equal amount of carbonated water and serve. A slice of lemon or lime make a beautiful decoration for your iced tea.

© Burke/Triolo

COUNTRY TEA BLEND

*2 tablespoons each
   lemon balm
   chamomile flowers
   peppermint*

MAY WINE

May wine is a traditional country beverage from Europe that has been served on May Day (May first) for centuries. Its flavoring comes from sweet woodruff, a pretty spring herb that can be used dried, or better yet, fresh from your garden.

1 gallon dry, white wine

2 cups sweet woodruff, chopped

12 ounces champagne or carbonated water (optional)

Chop the sweet woodruff and add to wine. Let sit for at least two weeks, then strain. Champagne or carbonated water can be added just before serving.

Variations: Serve the wine in a bowl with flowers of sweet woodruff, borage, pansy, violets, or other spring blooms floating in it. Other herbs, such as borage, violet, and elder flowers, lemon and mint leaves, and clary sage bowes used instead of sweet woodruff create different-flavored wines.

EDIBLE FLOWER SALADS

Your country herb garden, as well as your flower garden, offers many edible flower snacks for color and variety, and some unique flavors. Use edible flowers in soups, floral salads, for floating in a punch bowl, or for decorating a cake.

© Brian Leatart

EIGHTEEN HERBS TO GROW FOR COOKING

Basil (*Ocimum basilicum*): annual
Bay (*Laurus nobilis*): perennial, not hardy
Chervil (*Anthriscus cerefolium*): annual
*Chives (*Allium schoenoprasum*): annual
*Coriander (*Coriandrum sativum*): annual
*Dill (*Anethum graveolens*): annual
*Garlic (*Allium sativum*): annual
Horseradish (*Armoracia rusticana*): perennial
Marjoram (*Origanum vulgare*): perennial
Oregano (*Origanum vulgare*): perennial
Parsley (*Petroselinum crispum*): biennial
Rosemary (*Rosemarinus officinalis*): perennial
Sage (*Salvia officinalis*): perennial
*Salad Burnet (*Poterium sanguisorba*): perennial
Savory, summer (*Saturia hortensis*): annual
Sorrel, French (*Rumex scutatus*): perennial
Tarragon, French (*Artemisia dracunculus sativa*): perennial
Thyme (*Thymus vulgaris*): perennial

*Edible flowers. Some other edible flowers include: clove pinks, elder, lemon, mallow, pansy, and roses.

Coriander is one of the most popular culinary herbs in the world.

Marjoram is often confused with oregano, but it gives its own delightfully distinctive taste to foods.

EIGHTEEN HERBS TO GROW FOR TEA

*Borage (*Borago officinalis*): annual
*Calendula (*Calendula officinalis*): annual
 Catnip (*Nepeta cataria*): perennial
 Chamomile, German (*Matricaria recutita*): annual
*Geranium (*Pelargonium* species): perennial, not hardy
 Lemon balm (*Melissa officinalis*): perennial
*Peppermint (*Mentha piperita*): perennial
 Spearmint (*Mentha spicata*): perennial
*Sweet woodruff (*Galium odorata*): perennial
*Violet (*Viola odorata*): perennial

*Edible flowers. Some other edible flowers include: clove pinks, elder, lemon, mallow, pansy, and roses.

© Rogers Associates

The pleasing lemony taste of lemon balm (above) or chamomile (below) make a delicious tea.

© Derek Fell

FRAGRANCE IN YOUR LIFE

Most people are intrigued with fragrance. It affects their moods, recalls memories, and, in general, enriches their lives. No wonder country homes have used aromatic herbs for centuries. Your home, too, can come alive with inviting aromas from potpourri jars, pillows, pomanders, and incense of special-smelling blends.

POTPOURRI

Potpourri is a blend of fragrant and attractive dried plants. There are many recipes available, but I encourage you to learn the true art of potpourri making by creating your own blends. Potpourri is translated from the French as a "combination of diverse elements," and it is diversity that gives the blend character.

Like perfume, individual scents are slightly elusive because they become a harmonious blend—a true potpourri of fragrance. Many plants lose their scent and color no matter how carefully they are dried, so try a few samples first. Some delicate flowers that will not keep their color or fragrance if air dried can be successfully dried in silica gel, as explained in Chapter Three.

Not all potpourri ingredients need to be fragrant. Similar to herb garden or herbal wreath design, a good potpourri is visually appealing because it incorporates contrasting colors and textures. Color can be subtle—pale shades of pink roses with lavender, or bright, with red roses, green cedar leaves, and yellow calendula petals.

Plants from your herb garden and from the wild provide the choicest potpourri materials. Most potpourri ingredients are herbal or floral, but any plant material that dries with an interesting fragrance, color, or texture is suitable. Mosses and lichens, small cones, or evergreen leaves are a few of the materials you may find beyond your garden fence. Materials can also be purchased if you need more variety. Visit a store that sells bulk herbs and let your eyes and nose choose for you.

ESSENTIAL OILS

Potpourri may be enhanced with fragrant essential oils. The fragrance of old-fashioned potpourri depended exclusively on aromatic herbs and flowers, but modern potpourri makers almost always use essential oils. When using essential oils, remember that you are only trying to bring out the herb's true fragrance, not overpower it. Start with small batches, adding essential oils drop by drop, until you get the smell of it. Keep a record of how many drops you use so you can duplicate your best creations later. Formulas may still need some adjustments, since essential oils vary greatly in quality and strength. Quality may be difficult to judge at first, but your skill will develop with practice.

FIXATIVES

Fixative herbs make a potpourri's fragrance last longer. Unlike most herbs, whose fragrance declines with time, fixatives improve their scent, and the scent of the entire potpourri, as they age.

Orris root (an iris you can grow in your herb garden) is the most popular fixative because its light, violetlike scent is not overpowering. It comes powdered, in chunks, and sometimes whole. Small, white chunks are preferred, since potpourri ingredients lose their luster when coated with orris powder.

Other fixatives include patchouli, sandalwood, vetiver, balsam of Peru, and gum benzoin, all available as dried herbs or essential oils. Another fixative, tonka bean, is sold

whole or chopped. The mild scent of sandalwood and the vanilla-like benzoin, balsam of Peru, or tonka bean easily blend into potpourri, while patchouli and vetiver must be added carefully. The heavy, earthy smell of these last two herbs is one that people either love or hate. Cleveland sage, a fragrant cousin of culinary sage, is another fixative. Although not usually commercially available, it will readily grow in your herb garden.

© Derek Fell

BASIC POTPOURRI

2 cups dried herbs

2 tablespoons orris root (or other fixative), chopped (for powdered orris root, or other fixature, use 1 tablespoon)

½ teaspoon essential oil blend

Combine the ingredients and let them sit one week in a closed container to develop the fragrance, which grows richer as it ages. Potpourri keeps fragrant for a few years closed in a container and lasts for months when used as a room freshener. When it finally begins to lose its scent, recharge it with essential oils. Sprinkling brandy on a potpourri is an old technique used to bring out its hidden fragrance.

Variation: Instead of blending the ingredients, layer in a clear glass jar.

© Robert Perron

COUNTRY GARDEN POTPOURRI

1 cup lemon verbena leaves, cut

1 cup calendula flower petals

½ cup Cleveland sage leaves, whole

¼ cup peppermint leaves, cut

¼ cup ammobium flowers, whole

¼ cup coriander seeds, whole

2 tablespoons orris root, chunks

½ teaspoon sandalwood essential oil

⅛ teaspoon clary sage essential oil

FLORAL BOUQUET POTPOURRI

1½ cups pink rose buds

½ cup lavender flowers, whole

½ cup rosemary leaves, whole

½ cup pink globe amaranth flowers, whole

¼ cup pearly everlasting flowers, whole

¼ cup clove pinks, petals

2 tablespoons orris root, chunks

¼ teaspoon bergamot essential oil

⅛ teaspoon rose geranium essential oil

¼ teaspoon lavender essential oil

WINTER SPICE POTPOURRI

½ cup red rose buds

½ cup uva ursi leaves, whole

¼ cup cedar leaves, cut

¼ cup cinnamon sticks, broken

⅛ cup juniper berries, whole

⅛ cup orange peel, pieces

⅛ cup star anise, whole

⅛ cup red rose hips, whole

2 tablespoons orris root

¼ teaspoon orange essential oil

⅛ teaspoon cinnamon essential oil

⅛ teaspoon clove essential oil

SACHETS

Grind a potpourri into powder and it becomes a sachet. Sewn or tied into cloth bags, sachets often find a home in the linen or lingerie drawer, where they lightly scent sheets and clothes. Sachets enclosed in envelopes can be tucked into letters and packages. Your cat will apppreciate a cat-nip sachet ball on a string. Moth-repellent sachets are eco-logical replacements for toxic, smelly mothballs. For the best-quality sachets, grind the potpourri yourself; herbs that are already ground will have lost much of their scent.

MOTH-REPELLING SACHET

2 tablespoons each
 cedar chips
 lavender flowers
 rosemary leaves
 wormwood leaves

½ teaspoon cedar essential oil

Combine ingredients, grind or blend, and tie into sachet balls. Each one-inch sachet ball replaces one mothball. Lightly crush the bags to release more scent. Recharge them with essential oils every year or two.

Variations: The leaves of bay, patchouli, costmary, peppermint, rosemary, rue, southernwood, and sassafras are also used to repel clothes moths, so use whatever your herb garden provides. For extra-strength balls, add ⅛ teaspoon camphor essential oil (nonsynthetic).

BASIC SACHET

2 cups potpourri

Grind the potpourri in a coffee grinder or blender. Store in a sealed jar or bag for one week to allow the fragrance to completely permeate the ground herbs.

SACHET BALLS

1 tablespoon powdered sachet

6-inch square of fabric

8 inches ribbon or string

To make sachet balls, cut the fabric with pinking shears. (Choose thin fabric with a tight weave to contain the powder.) Place a heaping tablespoon of the sachet powder in the center, bring the corners together, and tie them with ribbon or string.

STOVE-TOP POTPOURRI

A tablespoon of stove-top potpourri (also known as sim-mering potpourri) fills the house with wafting herbal fra-grances when simmered in water. You can buy ceramic potpourri cookers that have bowls heated by a candle or electricity. Stove-top potpourri can also be simmered in a pan of water placed on a wood stove or other heat source. These potpourri rely mostly on essential oils for their lasting power. It is easy to turn any potpourri into a stove-top version simply by increasing the quantity of essential oils.

BASIC STOVE-TOP POTPOURRI

2 cups potpourri

2 teaspoons essential oil blend
 (your choice)

POTPOURRI PILLOWS

Potpourri-filled pillows can be simple gingham squares or fancy satin and velvet pillows with ribbons and lace edgings. It was once common to stuff bed pillows with herbs to enhance sleeping. "Dilly" pillows, filled with dill seeds and other herbs, were put in cradles to lull babies to sleep. Victorian women used to land on lavender-filled "swooning" pillows to help revive them when they fainted.

Fill pillows with herbs instead of stuffing them. Throw pillows are too heavy and lumpy when stuffed completely with herbs; instead insert a thin, herb pillow of muslin next to the regular batting. (Sew baffles in the inner pillow—as on a comforter—to keep the herbs from shifting.) A potpourri-filled hot pad produces wonderful fragrances every time a hot pan is laid on it.

DREAM PILLOWS

A sleep pillow, to be placed under your bed pillow, can be small. I make mine five by four inches. Hops encourage sleep. Turn sleep into dreams by adding mugwort, which has a reputation for instilling dreams. Lavender is said to make dreams pleasant and thyme to prevent nightmares. To recall dreams, Shakespeare suggested, "Rosemary, that is for remembrance." Include roses for dreams of love and everlasting flowers to ensure that love lasts forever.

Your friends will appreciate receiving dream (or love) pillows, especially if you enclose a card explaining the old traditions. Refer to old herbals for more ideas. When giving someone a dream pillow, you might enclose a blank journal so they can record their wonderful herbal dreams.

BASIC PILLOW INGREDIENTS

$\frac{1}{2}$ *cup hops*

$\frac{1}{4}$ *cup lavender flowers*

$\frac{1}{8}$ *cup rosemary leaves*

$\frac{1}{8}$ *cup thyme leaves*

2 tablespoons mugwort leaves

Blend ingredients and sew into small pillows.

© Anita Sabarese

Europeans have slept on pillows stuffed with hops since medieval days to encourage restful sleep.

© William Adams

There are over 100 different varieties of thyme you can grow in your garden.

MOIST POTPOURRI

Moist potpourri are a blend of herbs and flowers that are only partially dried so they remain slightly moist. They use salt to absorb the moisture and fragrance of fresh herbs and flowers. This method preserves many herbal scents that would be lost if the plants were air-dried. Fresh potpourri can be an ongoing project. Add to it as you harvest plants throughout the year.

BASIC RECIPE

2 cups potpourri herbs, fresh

1 cup table salt, without iodine

¼ cup orris root, powdered (optional)

wide-mouthed jar or small crock

wooden mallet or spoon

Dry herbs for a couple days, until limp. Place about ½ inch of herbs in the bottom of a crock or jar. Pound them flat with a wooden mallet (or a thick wooden spoon). Cover the herbs with a ⅛-inch layer of salt. Add another layer of herbs and salt, and pound again. Repeat this process until all the materials have been used. Let sit for at least five days, then stir. Continue to stir every three days for about a month.

© Tony Cenicola

© Anita Sabarese

LAVENDER WANDS

Lavender buds keep their scent for years when kept in these wands. When they do begin to lose their scent, you can gently crush them to release the fragrance and memories of a summer herb garden. People love these wands, but they always ask me what to do with them. Popular in the Victorian era, they were used like sachets.

If you are like me, you may be too busy in the summer garden to complete this project right away. The stalks can be secured with a rubber band while they dry, then put away to wait for a lazy winter day.

LAVENDER WANDS

fresh lavender stalks

rubber bands

1 yard satin ribbon, ⅛-inch thick

Cut thirteen fresh lavender bud stalks from your garden just before the buds open. This is generally in July or August, when lavender is most fragrant. Carefully bend the stems over, just below the flowering heads. Insert the end of a ⅛-inch satin ribbon into the buds. Weave the ribbon through the stalks, going under one, over the next, and under again, keeping it tight enough to enclose the buds. Continue weaving down the stalk. Tie off with a knot and make a pretty bow. The lavender wand will bulge over the buds and the stalks will form a handle.

© Anita Sabarese

ROSE POMANDERS

Rose pomanders can only be described as beautiful. They literally stop traffic at craft fairs. The technique is not difficult, but it does require patience and a supply of tight rosebuds. If you do not have a rose border around your herb garden, order buds through an herb supplier. First clean the buds by removing loose or discolored outer petals and discolored or broken buds. (Save rejects for potpourri.)

2 ounces rose buds (about 120 buds)

white glue

2-inch Styrofoam ball

2- to 6¼-inch lace and/or satin ribbons, 12 inches long

2 inches florist wire

Make a ¼-inch-deep hole in the Styrofoam ball with the tip of a pencil (or other pointed instrument). Dab in a drop of glue and gently press the base of a rosebud into the hole. Continue, closely staggering the buds so no Styrofoam shows between them, until the ball is covered. Leave a ½-inch space for ribbons.

Twist the wire around the center of the ribbons to secure them. Put a dab of glue in the space reserved and push the wire's ends into the ball. The ribbons can be tied into bows or loops or left to cascade over the pomander. Use one set of ribbons to hang the pomanders. For a final touch, dried flowers can be glued around the top of the ball, encircling the ribbons.

To retain its scent and color, hang your pomander out of direct sun or fluorescent lights. Dab with rose essential oil or your favorite potpourri oil blend if you need to recharge the fragrance in future years.

© Bruce McCandless

POTPOURRI BALL

This ball is a hanging potpourri, so use a colorful potpourri mix. Hang one anywhere to add color and fragrance to your home.

2-inch Styrofoam ball

white glue

1 to 2 tablespoons potpourri

¼-inch ribbons

Chop the herbs into fine, uniform pieces, about ⅛-inch long, in a blender or coffee grinder. Dip the ball into white glue and spread the glue thinly over half the surface. Sprinkle potpourri over the glue until covered. Let dry, then glue and sprinkle the other side of the ball. When dry, leave the potpourri ball as is, or give it a polished look with hairspray or lacquer. Insert ribbon to hang and decorate as described for rose pomanders.

SCENTED BEADS

Scented beads can be worn like jewelry, hung as small pomanders, kept in a bowl as room fresheners, or tossed in drawers to scent clothes. They can also be heated in a simmering pan of water or thrown in the fire to scent the house. Some of the first rosaries were made from beads whose scent was released as they were handled.

Scented beads are fun to make, and so easy that they are a great project for children who will want to wear them and share them with friends. The bead "clay" can be rolled into round beads or patted into squares, rectangles, triangles, medallions, or any shape you can imagine.

1 tablespoon gum tragacanth, powdered

1 tablespoon gum benzoin, powdered

1 tablespoon orris root, powdered

1 tablespoon lavender flowers, powdered

about 4 tablespoons water

½ teaspoon essential oils (your choice)

Mix the herbs, add the essential oils, and stir in enough water to make a paste with the consistency of stiff cookie dough. Form this "clay" into shapes. Pierce with a large needle or wire for beads. Place the beads on waxed paper and let them harden for few days. (A low heat source quickens the drying time.) The finished beads will be so hard they can even be sanded smooth.

Variations: Replace the lavender with another aromatic herb. Rose or orange water (available at most liquor stores), vanilla, peppermint, or orange extract (from the grocery store), or strong herb tea can replace the water for added fragrance. If gum tragacanth is difficult to find, the formula can be made without it, but it will be more crumbly.

HERBAL INCENSE

Burning small amounts of incense will fill your house with a lasting fragrance. You can make quality incenses with all your favorite fragrances.

Potassium nitrate, also called saltpeter, ignites the incense, and charcoal keeps it burning. Charcoal capsules (open them up) and potassium nitrate are both sold at drug stores. You can also powder the charcoal blocks sold to burn as incense. The charcoal is messy to work with, but it washes off easily.

2 tablespoons gum tragacanth

1 tablespoon gum benzoin

1 tablespoon charcoal

1 teaspoon potassium nitrate

1 teaspoon essential oils (your choice)

4 tablespoons water

Mix the powders together. Add the essential oils and enough water to make a paste. Form into small cones, about one inch tall, and set on waxed paper until dry. Light and enjoy!

To make incense sticks, form the paste into a five-inch-long roll. Stick a lavender stalk (without the flower head), or other small stick, into the paste and form the paste around it. It is easier to form a triangular shape than a round roll around the stick. Place on waxed paper for a few days to dry.

TEN HERBS TO GROW FOR FRAGRANCE

Chamomile, Roman (*Chamaemelum nobile*): perennial
Clove pinks (*Dianthus carophyllus*): perennial
Geraniums (*Pelargonium* species): perennial, not hardy
Lavender (*Lavandula angustifolia*): perennial
Lemon verbena (*Aloysia triphylla*): perennial, not hardy
Orris (*Iris florentina*): perennial
Rose (*Rosa* species): perennial
Sage, clary (*Salvia sclarea*): biennial
Sage, Cleveland (*Salvia clevelandia*): perennial
Violets (*Viola odorata*): perennial

Chamomile is enjoyed as a fragrant herb and tea throughout the world.

Even a small patch of violets fill the early spring garden with their heavenly aroma.

© Christopher Bain

CHAPTER SEVEN

PRESSED HERBS AND FLOWERS

Pressing herbs and flowers preserves nature's colors and forms and provides another way to bring your garden and the countryside into your home. Pressed plants can decorate wall hangings, book covers, boxes, furniture, or any other flat surface. They make very special greeting or note cards from your garden. Use them when you give any of the gift ideas in this book and for any special occasions. They can also decorate name tags and stationery.

I press flowers not only for their beauty, but to keep a record of herbs that grow in different places. These flower journals bring back wonderful memories of Grecian hillsides blanketed with flowers, the highlands of Guatemala, and backpacking in the High Sierra.

Once you start pressing flowers, you will see plants to collect everywhere you go. Although the technique is commonly called flower pressing, any interesting part of the plant can be used. Part of the fun of plant drying is to see how each plant is transformed when pressed. Be prepared for some colors to fade either during pressing or after they are dried, but even then, most dried plants keep their charm. The only plants to avoid are those that are poisonous.

PRESSING FLOWERS

Any book will press flowers but, even when protected with newspaper, pages may become stained and warped. The absorbent pages of an old phone book make a quick press, although dried flowers easily break if the book is bent. A spiral notepad is a handy press on nature walks since notes can be jotted down right next to plants taped on its pages. Children enjoy making their own flower books during family outings and vacations. When you get home, place the notepad under a stack of books for pressing.

Plants must be pressed fresh. Collect them when they are as dry as possible and dust off any pollen, bugs, or dirt. If you gather flowers while strolling along a country lane and your bouquet wilts on the way home, set it in a vase of water to perk it up before drying.

Manicure scissors, X-Acto™ knives, and tweezers are helpful tools of the flower-pressing trade. Pick flowers very carefully, by their stem whenever possible, since delicate ones can bruise just from handling. Fat plant parts, such as thick buds, stems, and leaf ribs need to be sliced in half so the plant can lie flat. Take off a back section, since it won't be seen.

Carefully lay out the flowers so they do not overlap another plant or themselves, unless you purposely want this special effect. Small pieces of nonpermanent, clear tape (available at office-supply stores) will help hold down sturdy stems and leaves. Some flower parts are easier to press separately, then reconstruct later. Flower clusters also need to be pressed individually. For variety, press some flowers with a "profile" instead of open faced and bend some stems into graceful curves. Be sure to press more plants than you need so you have a good selection from which to choose.

The beautiful form and thin petals of violets make them perfect specimens for pressing.

MOUNTING PRESSED PLANTS

Once dry, pressed plants are very delicate and feather light. Transport them with tweezers or on small slips of paper, being careful that they don't fly around the room. They can be stored on sheets of cardboard in a box. Keep a list of the flowers it contains so you can quickly locate the ones you want.

A storage method I learned from Milaika Edwards, a creative fourteen-year-old who has been drying flowers for years, is a "magnetic" photo album with self-stick pages. The stiff pages are covered with clear plastic to protect the flowers and make it easy to flip through the book to select them. You do need to carefully peel the clear pages back so the flowers don't break. Avoid putting very thin, delicate flowers in the album, since they tend to adhere to the sticky pages and break.

Small drops of rubber cement will secure dried flowers to their permanent surface. (White glue wrinkles the plants and paper as it dries.) Make sure the cement doesn't get on the plant's surface. When the completed "flower picture" is dry, you can cover it with clear contact paper or shellac, or place in a glass-covered picture frame. If you have access to a laminating machine, it can be used to protect the plants.

You can protect your flowers by either spraying on a clear-drying fixative or painting a clear-drying preservative over them. (Both are available at craft, hobby, and art stores.) Use a very soft bristled brush when painting on a preservative and work carefully to avoid breaking the plants. This technique is particularly handy when making a project where you don't want to cover the entire sheet with plastic, but do need to protect the flowers. In a pinch, if you can't find the right materials or you want an inexpensive protection of children's projects, you can brush on a thin layer of white glue.

One way to display and protect your floral pictures is to frame and hang them on the wall. Buy a wooden or plastic frame with a plate glass insert designed for framing photo-

graphs. Select a heavy paper that does not bend too easily and cut it to fit in the frame. Follow the instructions for mounting pressed flowers on paper. When the flowers are dry, place the picture in the frame and fasten on the back of the frame to secure it. Your floral picture is ready to hang and enjoy for years to come. The color of some of the flowers may fade with time, but they will keep their delicate form and beauty. The colors will last longer if kept out of direct sunlight.

PRESSED FLOWER CARDS

Quality paper for making your own cards is available from craft, stationery, or gift stores, or from a printer. Matching envelopes are often available. Before folding the card, "score" it by running the scissor blade lightly along a ruler to slightly indent (not cut) the paper where you want the fold. Fold the paper away from the dent to make a nice even crease that doesn't buckle. Pressed flowers can be glued with rubber cement directly onto the card or onto another piece of paper that is then glued onto the card.

Once the dried flowers are on the card, they are still very delicate and can easily be damaged. To protect them, let the glue dry, then cover them with a piece of clear contact paper. (Contact paper is sold at variety stores and at some grocery and hobby stores). Cut the contact paper exactly the size of the front of the card. Peel the backing off the sticky side and lay one edge along the matching edge of the flower picture. Allow the contact paper to roll down inch by inch until the picture is completely covered. Gently press down any air pockets that are left around the flowers. Applying contact paper smoothly may take some practice, so try it on a few samples until you get the hang of it.

© Christopher Bain

FLOWER MOBILES

A unique way to display dried flowers is to make a double-sided card and hang them individually or as a mobile. Children seem to be especially fond of flower mobiles. They also provide a visual decoration for people who are bedridden. Small dried flower cards can be hung almost anywhere, including the Christmas tree.

Cut a stiff card in the shape or shapes you prefer (but don't fold it in half). Glue flowers on the one side, let dry, then cover with clear contact paper. Glue flowers on the opposite side, let dry, and cover them with contact paper. You will have a double-sided card that can twirl and display the flowers. Another version, but one that takes a steady hand, places the pressed flowers directly on a piece of clear contact paper and covers them with another sheet of contact paper. This way both the front and back of the flowers are visible. Since these are flexible, be careful not to bend them and break the flowers.

A more elaborate mobile can be made from glass. Purchase small, clear glass pieces from a craft store or a stained-glass supply store. Microscope slides (from a science-supply or hobby store) will also work. Cut the card the same size as the piece of glass. Glue pressed flowers to both sides and let dry. Lay the card on one piece of glass and cover with another piece exactly the same size, placing tiny dabs of glue around the inner edge of the glass to adhere it. The flower card will then be contained between two pieces of glass. To cover the rough edges and to provide a hanger, glue a cord (from the fabric store) all around the edge and make a loop at the top. If you prefer, the flowers can be glued directly onto one piece of glass; then glue the two pieces of glass together so both the front and back of the flowers are displayed and you can see through the glass. Very small glass can even be hung from earring wires or worn as a necklace.

Either of these techniques can be adapted to making pressed-flower kitchen magnets. Glue the flowers on a card and glue a piece of glass over them. Cut a stiff piece of cardboard into the same size and glue it to the back. Glue a magnet to the middle of the cardboard. (Small magnets and magnetic strips that can be cut to size are sold in craft and hardware stores.)

FLOWER PRESS

If you plan to do much plant pressing, buy a press or make your own. A homemade press uses blotting paper to absorb the plants' moisture, corrugated cardboard to increase air circulation for quick drying, and plywood ends bolted down to press the plants flat. You can make a flower press any size. A small press is convenient for children or to carry on hikes.

2 pieces plywood, 10 inches square

4½-inch bolts with wing nuts

8 pieces corrugated cardboard, 10 inches square

16 pieces blotter paper (or 32 pieces of newspaper), 10 inches square

paint or lacquer (optional)

mat knife or razor blade

drill

Drill a ¼-inch hole in each corner of the plywood, about three-quarters of an inch from each edge. The wood can be sanded, then painted or varnished if you wish. (Later, you might want to decorate the top with dried flowers.) Cut the corners off the cardboard sheets and blotting paper 1½ inches from each corner. Stack the cardboard pieces with two sheets of blotting paper between each one. (The flowers you want to dry will go in between the sheets of blotting paper.) Place the stack between the two sheets of plywood like a sandwich and bolt it together, with the bolts going through the holes in the plywood. The bolts should miss the cardboard and blotting paper where their corners have been cut off. The bolts need to be just tight enough to keep the layers of cardboard very flat. Keep the press in a warm place with good air circulation while the flowers are drying. The cardboard will keep air circulating in the rack.

MINI FLOWER PRESS

When you are out in the country, or any time carrying a press is impractical, use a mini press so you don't have to pass by a beautiful flower. Fasten a small stack of corrugated cardboard squares and blotting paper together with a heavy rubber band. When you get home, place it under a stack of books to finish pressing the flowers.

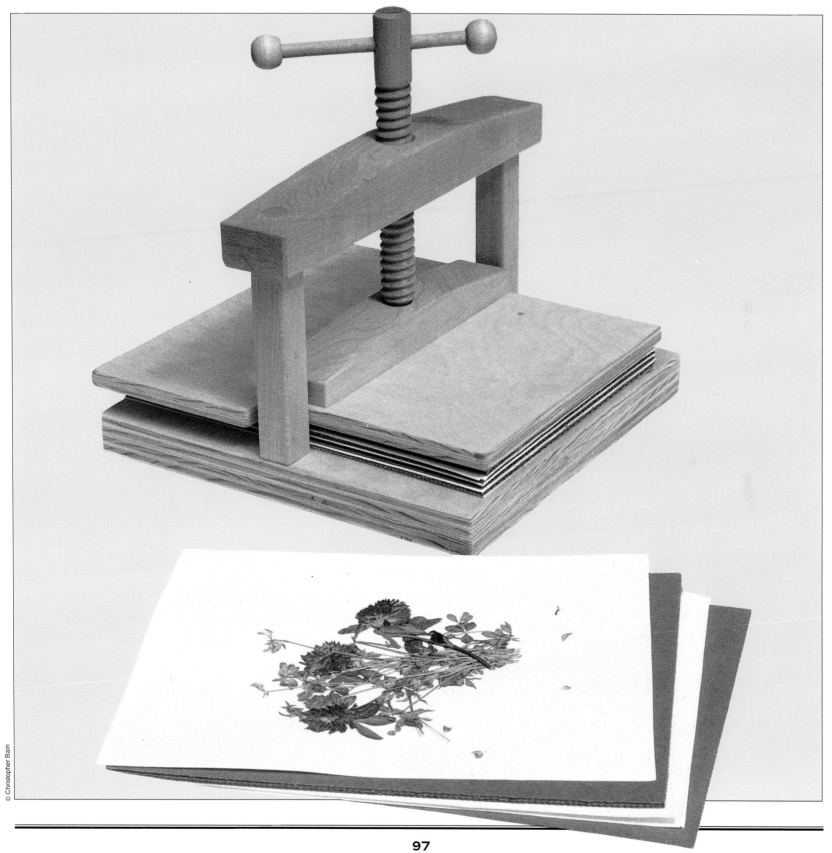

FOURTEEN FLOWERS TO GROW FOR PRESSING

Bleeding hearts (*Dicentra* species): perennial
Clematis (*Clematis* species): perennial
Coreopsis (*Coreopsis* species): annual; perennial
Echinacea (*Echinacea* species): perennial
Geraniums (*Pelargonium* species): perennial
Hellebore (*Heleborus* species): perennial
Hydranga (*Hydranga* species): perennial
Hypericum (*Hypericum* species): perennial
Larkspur (*Delphinium* species): annual; perennial
Lilys (*Lilium* species): perennial
Lobelia (*Lobelia* species): annual; perennial
Pansy (*Viola* species): perennial
Poppies (*Papaver* species): annual; perennial
Sage (*Salvia* species): annual; biennial; perennial

Flowers such as coneflower *(top)* **and pansies** *(bottom)* **retain their bright color even when pressed.**

CHAPTER EIGHT

HERBAL AND FLORAL WREATHS

Herbal and floral wreaths give any home a country feeling. They not only look nice, but they also carry light aromas of the herbs and flowers they contain. Make wreaths for the wall, small candle wreaths, or large wreaths to enclose a festive punch bowl or to use as a centerpiece. They can be draped in swags over windows and doors and even be worn on the head. Wreaths dress up weddings and birthdays and lend themselves to many other occasions.

Floral head wreaths are appropriate for any festive day. Head wreaths also look lovely as hatbands on straw hats. When not being worn, head wreaths can be used to decorate the wall. For weddings, they can be attached to the bride's veil. You can also make head wreaths for bridesmaids and flower girls (and matching corsages and boutonnieres and even dried flower bouquets).

Creating a wreath is one of the most rewarding of herbal crafts. Even those who describe themselves as "all thumbs" make absolutely beautiful wreaths. All you need are the right materials, a little time, and a few step-by-step instructions.

The plants for your wreath can be harvested from your herb and flower garden, collected in the wild, or purchased from nurseries. Cones, barks, nuts, mosses, and twigs that might otherwise be overlooked can accent your wreath. Even objects you might not think of as wreath materials, such as shells, dried chili peppers, small gourds, miniature corn on the cob, and various leaves can create fascinating wreaths. Always keep your eye out for interesting materials. Ribbons, small feathered birds (sold in craft stores), or other additions can be used.

Good sources for dried materials are craft and hobby stores (find them in the phone book). Farmer's markets, where local gardeners sell their produce, grocery stores, and shops at herb farms often sell fresh herbs and flowers that you can dry yourself, following the instructions in

Chapter Three. Dried or fresh plants can be used and even combined in the same wreath. A wreath made with fresh materials should be laid flat until it is dry, to prevent it from sagging as it dries.

The biggest problem for beginning wreath makers is using more material than is needed. The first wreath I made must have contained a quarter of my garden. It still hangs on my parents' wall and when I see it now, I realize it contains enough material to make a dozen wreaths.

Dried peppers provide intense color and intriguing shapes in this wreath.

© Robert Hoebermann

Using silica gel to dry flowers makes it possible to use a wide range of materials, such as violets, to accent a unique wreath.

© Robert Hoebermann

WREATH TECHNIQUE #1 STRAW-BASED WREATHS

The most common wreath-making technique uses a straw wreath base, purchased from a craft store. This technique is especially useful if you want a thick wreath that stands out from the wall or plan to cover it with heavy materials, such as cones. If you've seen straw bases and wondered how they manage to stay together, a Styrofoam core supports the flexible straw. The straw looks more natural, but a plain Styrofoam base works just as well. If you want to make sure a white Styrofoam base doesn't show through the herbs, buy a green one or spray-paint it before using.

10-inch straw or Styrofoam base

dried plants

wired sticks (from craft store)

spray fixative (optional)

Divide the plant materials you choose into thirty-six miniature bouquets, about 2 inches in diameter and 5 inches long, with about 2 inches of stems. The easiest design is to make twelve each of three different bouquets. Each style can be composed of all one plant or of different plants. Lay out the bouquets, but don't bother to tie them.

Most plant stems are too flimsy to directly stick into the base. Craft stores sell small wooden sticks with thin wires attached for winding the bouquet stems on the stick. You can then poke the stick into the base. There are also wreath-making machines that automatically attach the bouquet to a pointed metal stick. If you're making many wreaths at once, you can rent one of these machines from some craft stores. Another method uses metal pins (about the same length, but wider than bobby pins) that pin each bouquet on the base. Materials can also be glued on, although it takes a lot of glue, so most wreath makers reserve glue for final touch-ups.

Making the Wreath

Insert the bouquets into the wreath at an angle so they lie against the wreath base. They should all slant the same direction and overlap like feathers on a bird's back. Space the bundles evenly, just far enough apart so the base doesn't show through. You can work your way around the base in any direction, starting with the inside, outside, or top row first.

When the wreath is covered with flowers and herbs, stand back and admire your creation. Glue on any minor corrections and extra materials. Choose the best direction to hang the finished wreath. Then, make a hanger by twisting a short piece of florist wire into a loop around your finger. Turn the twisted wire ends into a J and insert it securely into the base and your wreath is ready to hang.

© Robert Hoebermann

WREATH TECHNIQUE #2 WIRE-BASED WREATHS

This is my favorite wreath technique because you make your own base, allowing more flexibility of size and shape. This technique uses about one-third of the amount of the materials as a straw-based wreath, so it ends up saving time and money.

Make a wreath base out of a heavy-gauge wire macrame ring sold in craft and hobby stores. These rings come in all sizes, so your wreath can be as large or as small as you wish. Specially made heart wires are also available. (You can make rings by bending heavy wire, from the hardware store, into a circle and soldering or wrapping the ends together.) I suggest not using coat hangers or other flexible wire because they are too flimsy. To wrap your wreath, use florist wire on a "paddle" or "spool" that is held in one hand, with the wire through your fingers. (Twenty-eight-gauge wire is flexible, but strong enough so it won't easily break.)

A possible disadvantage to the wire-based wreath is that you are limited to using plants that have flexible stems that won't snap off when wrapped with wire and tops that are full enough to give it width. German statice, sea lavender, airy baby's breath, fluffy pearly everlasting flowers, and gray wormwoods are a few excellent choices. Sweet Annie is popular, but has a notorious reputation for an allergic reaction. Moss works well, especially Spanish moss, which looks like lace. I also like grey santolina and the colorful annual statice, but use both of these fresh since they become too brittle when dried.

8-inch wire ring

dried plants

florist wire (28-gauge)

glue (optional)

spray fixative (optional)

The wreath base can be made from almost any flexible odds and ends from the garden that are not attractive enough for the wreath itself. Don't worry about its appearance, only the wall will see it! You can also use long pine needles, moss, or thin, flexible twigs. One of my favorite base materials is a stiff, long rush grass that grows wild in marshy areas where I live.

Fasten a bundle of the base plants (about ¾ to 1 inch thick) to the wire base by wrapping florist wire a couple of times around it. Twist the wire ends together to "knot" it and to tighten the plants on the ring. Continue wrapping the wire around the wreath with about a ½-inch space between each wrap, giving each a small tug to tighten it. At the end, overlap the plant material a little, then cut off any excess.

When the entire base is wrapped, cut the wire, leaving a few inches at the end.

© Robert Perron

Wrap this end under some wire that is already wrapped and twist the two together. Tuck this twisted wire away, down into the wreath.

Making the Wreath

Make each bouquet about 4 inches across and 5 inches long. An 8-inch ring takes twelve bouquets. Imagine a clock with twelve numbers and space them so each is on a number. Don't bunch them too tightly as many overzealous beginners, who discover they have used only eight of their twelve bouquets before they are halfway around the base do!

Wrap the bouquets onto the wreath base with florist wire, with the same technique used to wrap the base. Each bouquet requires about three wraps as you work down its stalk. Place the next bundle on top of the stems of the first bundle and wrap another three times. When the base is covered, cut the wire and twist it to "knot" it. At this stage, your wreath will look beautiful, but you can still glue on more material, even plants that are brittle or have no stems. This wreath can be hung on a push pin or small nail. Catch the inside of the ring on the nail or make a wire hanging loop (see Technique #1).

WREATH TECHNIQUE #3 HEAD WREATHS

The head-wreath technique is similar to that for a wire-based wreath, but it uses a flexible wire that adjusts to different head sizes. You can make a "headlet" to tie under the hair or partially encircle the head, with ribbons hanging on the side, or one that encircles the head, with ribbons hanging down the back.

Choose flexible plants that withstand an occasional bump without shattering, such as pearly everlasting, German statice, and sea lavender. Annual statice and baby's breath look beautiful on head wreaths but must be made flexible by being preserved with glycerine (described in Chapter Three). Since this wreath is designed to be worn, use florist tape, which is much more comfortable than wire.

flexible wire (from hardware store)

for a half wreath— 16 inches long

for a full wreath— 26 inches long

dried plants

florist tape, ¼-inch thick

white glue (optional)

spray fixative (optional)

ribbons

Wrap the entire length of the wire with florist tape to create a nonslippery surface. With pliers, twist the wire's ends into ¼-inch loops (for the ribbons). Make eight plant bouquets, about 2 inches across, for a half head wreath (or twelve for a full head wreath). Starting on one end, wrap the first bundle onto the wire with florist tape about three times. Place the next bundle facing the same direction so that it overlaps the stem of the first and wrap it. Continue along the wire until it is covered. Bend the wire carefully into a U. Tie matching ribbons through the loops and the wreath is ready to wear.

Dried swags offer a whole new dimension to interior design. Drape them over an arched entry, around a window, or to frame a baby crib.

© Robert Hoebermann

TECHNIQUE #4 DRIED FLOWER SWAGS

Swags are fashionable accessories for the country home. They can be hung looped on nails on the wall, placed along a bannister, or hung arching over a doorway, window, mirror, or picture frame. This technique wraps plant bouquets on a flexible rope instead of on a wire so the swag can be hung in graceful curves. The rope's length determines how long your swag will be. Be sure to use a good-quality, tightly woven rope (from a craft or hardware store).

rope, ¼-inch thick

dried plants

florist wire

glue (optional)

spray fixative (optional)

Make plant bouquets 4 to 6 inches across and 6 inches long. Wrap florist wire around each one to hold it together. Start at one end of the rope and wrap the first bundle securely with florist wire. Wrap the next bundle so it overlaps the stems of the first one, and proceed along the length of the rope until the swag is completed.

© Robert Hoebermann

FINISHING THE WREATHS
GLUING ACCESSORIES

As a last step, different materials can be glued onto any of your wreath projects. When making your first wreaths, you will have the best success by limiting the number of extra materials glued on. Choose perhaps four items; you can always add more later. Arrange them, then glue them on the wreath. When finished, hang your wreath and step back to check for places that need to be filled out.

You have your choice of white or hot glue. White glue takes a while to dry, but gives you plenty of time to change your mind. Hot glue dries instantly and is great as long as you work fast and are sure of placement. (If you do make a mistake, carefully cut pieces off instead of pulling them, and a quarter of the wreath, off the base.) One problem with hot glue is it leaves trails resembling spiderwebs.

Hot glue comes in two forms. Glue sticks are used in a glue gun that is very mobile, but leaves you with only one hand free. Hot melt glue chips are melted (use an old electric pan) and plant materials are dipped into it, which can be awkward, but leaves both hands free. In either case, be careful with the hot glue.

SPRAYING THE WREATHS

If you wish, wreaths can be sprayed with a fixative to extend their life and help keep tiny pieces intact. (Unless, of course, you make an edible herbal wreath for use in the kitchen!) Lacquer and shellac produce a slight sheen on pods and cones but don't change the appearance or fragrance of most herbs and flowers. Air out for twelve hours to get rid of the fumes. The most ecological method is to use ordinary hairspray, which is available in nonaerosol spray bottles.

Your wreath will keep for many years if it is hung away from direct sunlight and moisture. If you cannot resist hanging a wreath on your front door, bring it in for the winter. Or, since you know how to make them, replace your outdoor wreath with a new one every year.

FIFTEEN HERBS AND FLOWERS TO GROW FOR WREATHS

Amaranth (*Amaranthus caudatus*): annual
Ammobium (*Ammobium alatum*): perennial
Baby's breath (*Gypsophila paniculata*): perennial
Cupid's dart (*Catananche caerulea*): perennial
Globe amaranth (*Gomphrena* species): annual
Love-in-a-mist (*Nigella damascena*): annual
Safflower (*Carthamus tinctorius*): annual
Santolina, grey (*Santolina virens*): perennial
Sea holly (*eryngium* species): perennial
Statice, annual (*Limonium latifolium*): perennial
Statice, German (*Goniolimon tataricum*): perennial
Strawflower (*Helichrysum bracteatum*): annual
Tansy (*Tanacetum vulgare*): perennial
Wormwood (*Artemisia absinthium*): perennial
Yarrow (*Achillea* species): perennial

Tansies can be effectively grouped or placed individually on a wreath for a pleasant yellow accent.

Yarrow comes in white, pearl, gold, yellow, rose-pink, and deep red-pink. While the pink does not always hold its color, it does keep its attractive form.

HERBAL GIFTS FOR A COUNTRY CHRISTMAS

Winter in the country is a special time. The chores of harvesting herbs, preserving the garden's harvest, and cutting firewood are done. The time has come to enjoy the warmth of the wood stove and friends and to bring some cheer into winter's cold, short days. It also brings time to make gifts. When the holiday season arrives, they will only need the addition of a ribbon, then they can be sent on their way or placed under the tree.

If you want to have the most charming old-world Christmas imaginable, make your own herbal ornaments and gifts, for which recipes and projects abound in this chapter. The country Christmas tree is an old-fashioned tree, filled with handmade ornaments, candies, and little gifts hidden among the boughs. It may have small bunches of dried flowers and even candles. This is a tree of wonder and imagination that represents a lifestyle that takes time to create fantasies and gifts to share with friends.

ORNAMENTS
POMANDER BALLS

A pomander ball is a spicy, hanging potpourri made from an orange or other fruit studded with cloves. The cloves act as a wick to draw out the fruit juice and as natural preservatives to keep the fruit from spoiling as it dries. A spicy pomander powder covers the ball and preserves its aroma for years to come.

Oranges are the most popular fruit to use for pomander balls, but apples, lemons, limes, and even grapefruits, will work. Pomanders always make a nice gift, reminiscent of old-world charm. Hang them on the Christmas tree, use them in centerpieces, and tie them on packages. Pomanders take weeks to dry, so start this holiday project ahead of time.

Oranges or other fruit

Whole cloves

⅛-inch-thick ribbon

Cinnamon, powdered

Orris root, powdered

⅛-inch-thick strips of masking tape

Nail

In the "olden days," pomanders, made from oranges and cloves were considered very precious. Today, almost any fruit, from limes to apples, is used.

Placing cloves in an orange can be very time-consuming, so I space the cloves far apart and leave room for plenty of ribbon. It makes for a more attractive pomander with less work—a perfect combination!

Ribbons looks best lying flat against the fruit rather than over bumpy cloves, so reserve a space for them with the masking tape. Fill the space between the masking tape with cloves by first piercing the orange's skin with a nail (or other pointed object). Leave the space of one clove between each one. You can place the cloves closer, but not touching, or they will pop each other out when the orange shrinks from drying. While it is difficult to keep the little bud on the end of the clove, try not to break the star at the clove's base.

When the fruit is covered, peel off the masking tape and roll the clove-studded ball in the powdered herbs. Keep the pomander in a cardboard box or paper bag where there is warmth and good air circulation, such as on a high kitchen cabinet. Every day for the first week, roll it again in the powdered herbs. After a few weeks, it will be dry and very lightweight. Glue the ribbon in the space reserved for it. To dress up your pomander, glue on extra bows, ribbon streamers, and tiny dried flowers or spices.

Variations: Add $\frac{1}{8}$ teaspoon essential oils to the pomander powder before you roll the ball. You can also use other powdered herbs, like nutmeg and ginger, with or in place of the cinnamon. To hang, pomanders can be strung like beads if a hole is pierced all the way through before they are dry.

SPICE ORNAMENTS

Spices go so well with Christmas. No wonder these ornaments are so appealing. They look nice not only on the Christmas tree, but can be tied on gifts or evergreen wreaths and look great decorating a gift basket full of herbal presents. Their interesting shapes and entrancing smells result in all sorts of possibilities. Here are a few of my favorites. See what else you can come up with. They are easy to make and take very little time, so they are perfect projects for the kids.

cinnamon sticks, about 3 inches long

star anise

white glue or glue gun

ribbon

dried flowers

miniature birds (optional)

20-gauge florist wire (from the crafts store)

masking tape, ¼-inch wide

Technique I: Wrap four cinnamon sticks together with masking tape. Cover the tape with ribbon, gluing down the ends. Secure with a rubber band until dry. Glue a bow in the middle. Small dried flowers and spices can be glued around or on top of the bow. Loop a small string under the ribbon to hang.

Variations: Make attractive centerpieces for the Christmas table or the mantle by using ten large cinnamon sticks, 1

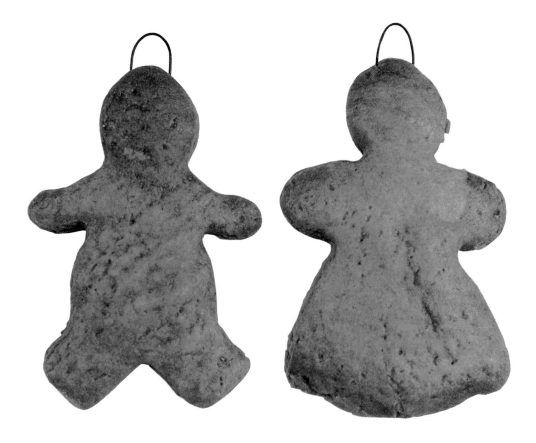

© Christopher Bain

or 2 feet long, wrapped with 2-inch-wide ribbon. After wrapping the sticks together, glue to keep them in place and decorate with cones and flowers.

Technique II: Slide a wire through three cinnamon sticks to form a triangle. Twist the wire's ends into a loop to hang. Glue a feathered bird and a few dried flowers in the center to create a "perch swing."

Technique III: Drill tiny holes through the ends of three cinnamon sticks. String the sticks together with a thin ribbon for hanging. Glue on extra bows.

"COOKIE" ORNAMENTS

These ornaments look and taste so good, you will have to remind everyone that they are not cookies.

¼ cup applesauce

½ cup cinnamon, powdered

2 tablespoons orris root, powdered

¼ teaspoon essential oils (optional)

Mix ingredients to the consistency of stiff cookie dough. Roll into a flat sheet. Cut into shapes with cookie cutters or a knife and make a hole at the top. Let dry for about four days. Drying time can be hastened by placing the ornaments near a heat source. When dry, put small strings through the hole and hang. The "cookies" can be frosted with a coat of paint and decorated by gluing on whole spices.

Variation: If you have apple pulp left over from making apple juice or jelly, replace the applesauce with about ½-cup pulp.

MINIATURE WREATHS

Miniature wreaths, only a few inches wide, can be made on a wooden ring—the kind used to hang draperies. Find them at craft and hardware stores. I save tiny flowers leftover from wreath and potpourri making for this project.

Miniature wreaths are ideal to tie on gifts, hang on the tree, or display on the wall. A small magnet (available at craft and hardware stores) glued on the back makes your wreath into a refrigerator magnet. These wreaths are also the perfect size for taper-candle wreaths. Make a pair and give them as a gift with a set of candles color coordinated to the wreaths. When the taper is placed in a candle holder, the wreath slides down over the top and is supported on the holder.

1 wood ring, 2 to 4 inches wide

dried flowers

glue

Glue the flowers on one side of the wooden ring. Let the glue dry and the wreath is finished. It's as simple as that.

© Brian Leatart

TASTY CHRISTMAS TREATS

HOLIDAY SPICE CAKE

Christmas isn't complete without a sweet treat. This cake has become a winter holiday tradition in my home, but its popularity is not limited to festive occasions. I serve it to any guest who happens by during the holidays and in my old-fashioned Christmas herb classes.

1½ cups flour

¼ teaspoon salt

2 teaspoons baking soda

¼ cup molasses

¼ cup brown sugar or honey

¼ cup butter

1 egg

⅔ cup milk

1 teaspoon lemon peel, grated

1 tablespoon holiday spice blend (see below)

Sift flour, salt, and baking soda together. Add molasses, brown sugar, or honey and warmed butter gradually, creaming them into the mix. Beat egg, add milk, lemon, and spice blend and add to mix. Stir batter until smooth. Spread into a greased pan (9 square inches or equivalent). Bake at 350°F for about thirty minutes.

Frost the cake while still warm with honey frosting (see below). For an added festive touch, decorate it with sliced persimmon or other fruit. You also can bake this cake in a round pan without a center and fill the center with green mint ice cream and red raspberries.

HOLIDAY SPICE BLEND

Holiday spice is an all-around, versatile blend that can be used not only in cakes, but for muffins, cookies, fruit dishes, or any dish needing a holiday flavor.

1 tablespoon each
cinnamon
orange peel

2 teaspoons each
allspice
anise
coriander

1 teaspoon each
cloves
ginger
nutmeg

Mix ground ingredients.

HONEY FROSTING

½ cup honey

3 ounces cream cheese

1 tablespoon milk

1½ teaspoons lemon peel, grated

1 teaspoon vanilla

Warm honey and blend all ingredients.

SPICED PEARS

Spiced fruit was once reserved for holidays or royalty, because spices were too expensive for everyday use. Today, we can enjoy a king's dish any day.

1 quart pears, cut

2 teaspoons holiday spice blend

Mix the spices and pears.

Variations: Try other types of fruit and fruit combinations. Use two tablespoons whole or chopped spices when canning fruit.

© Burke/Triolo

MULLING MIX

Mulled cider and wine were once the rage in England's country homes. The seventeenth century poet, John Gay, said, "Drink new cider, mulled with ginger, warm." Mulling herbs fill the house with holiday aromas, managing to make even the simplest occasion festive. At a party, you will notice people taking deep breaths as they comment, "Mmmm, that smells like Christmas!"

Serve mulled drinks to company and your family not only during the holiday season, but throughout the winter. Use sweet, red wine, apple cider, or any fruit juice or juice blend. The spices used were traditionally varied in view of what was available, so change the proportions to suit your taste. A bag or jar of mulling spices, decorated with a bow and a few cinnamon sticks, along with a bottle of wine, makes a special hostess gift.

4 sticks of cinnamon, 3 inches long*

2 heaping tablespoons dried orange peel, chopped

2 heaping tablespoons star anise, whole

1 tablespoon allspice, whole*

2 teaspoons cloves, whole*

1 teaspoon ginger powder

1 teaspoon nutmeg powder*

Combine ingredients and use one tablespoon of the mixture for every quart of wine or juice. Sweeten with two tablespoons of sugar or honey, if you wish. Gently simmer for about fifteen minutes. Heating removes wine's alcohol so if you want your drink to keep its punch, make a double batch of mulled wine (one teaspoon spices per pint), then dilute it with unheated wine before serving. Strain and serve warm.

Mulling herbs look great floating around in the pot, but to avoid having to strain the herbs before serving, put them in a cloth "mulling" bag during cooking. Buy a muslin bag with a drawstring top or tie the herbs in a cheesecloth sac. By the way, dry fresh orange peel by chopping the fresh (unsprayed) peel into ½-inch squares, and placing it in a warm place until it is dry.

Variations: For a simple mulling mix, use only the starred (*) items.

© Derek Fell

BATH GIFTS

Body-care products make wonderful, personal gifts that people can pamper themselves with again and again. Most of these are amazingly easy to make, but your friends and family won't believe it. Don't tell them it only took you ten minutes to make the elegant bath oil; we will keep it a secret.

Taking a fragrant herbal bath is a totally luxurious experience. It warms up cold winter days and drives away holidays pressures. This is a perfect gift if you are someone who has decided to make all your gifts, and it is already Christmas Eve. As long as you have the supplies on hand, you can have your gifts done in thirty minutes. Then, wrap them up and enjoy the evening, giving yourself a pat on the back for your creativity.

© Rogers Assoc.

Calendula flowers have been used in body-care products for centuries for their skin-soothing properties.

BATH HERBS

In this formula, the salt softens the water while the oatmeal turns it into a skin-softening, milky cream. Essential oils and herbs provide fragrance. The combination creates a creamy, herbal-scented, skin-softening solution every time you squeeze the bath bag. These bath bags can be used in place of soap, so they are good for those with sensitive skin, or for anyone who enjoys bathing.

For a gift, fill a fancy bottle with the bath herbs. A bag tied with a string or ribbon or with a drawstring is handy to fill and refill. Make the bag out of cotton or terry cloth, or get one of the muslin, drawstring bags (available at many natural food stores).

¼ cup each
   calendula flowers
   chamomile flowers
   lavender flowers

½ cup quick-cooking oatmeal

½ cup table salt

2 teaspoons lavender oil

a small bag

Combine ingredients and put ¼ cup in a small, cloth bag, about four inches square. Use for two to three baths, then refill the bag.

Variations: Use different herbs (almost any potpourri combination will work) or another oil or an oil blend instead of lavender.

HONEY-VANILLA LIP BALM

½ cup almond oil

½ ounce beeswax

1 teaspoon honey

1 tablespoon vanilla extract (from the grocery store)

Warm the oil just enough to melt the beeswax. Stir, and remove from heat. Stir in other ingredients. Pour immediately into small containers and let cool to harden.

The small plastic containers that lip balm are usually sold in are available in most backpacking supply stores. For an assortment of fancier containers, both import and cosmetic stores carry small containers made out of plastic, glass, or ceramic.

BATH OIL

2 ounces vegetable oil (your choice)

¼ teaspoon of lavender oil

Mix the oils and stir. It's done—really. If you are mailing it, don't even bother to stir it, the postal service will do that for you. Make fancy bath oil by adding a small dried flower sprig to each bottle. Either tie the sprig on the outside with ribbon or submerge it in the bath oil.

© Anita Sabarese

SCENTED BODY POWDER

½ cup arrowroot powder

½ cup cornstarch

2 tablespoons orris root, powdered

¼ teaspoon each carnation and violet essential oils

Combine the powders in a plastic bag, tie the bag well and mix by turning the bag over a few times. Add the essential oils to the powder, drop by drop. Break up any clumps that form. Let sit for at least five days while the scent spreads throughout the powder. Use as body, bath, or baby powder.

Place the finished body powder in a wide powder container and apply with a puff. For a shaker container, use a spice jar with a perforated lid insert or the shaker containers sold for salt, pepper, and sugar. (Containers are available in import and housewares stores or look for ceramic containers at craft fairs and handicraft stores.)

The scent of violets has been a favorite scent for body powders since Napoleon and Josephine brought it into fashion.

TWENTY USEFUL ESSENTIAL OILS

Benzoin	Lime
Bergamot	Orange
Cedarwood	Patchouli
Cinnamon	Peppermint
Clary sage	Petrigrain
Clove	Pine
Ginger	Rose geranium
Grapefruit	Rosemary
Lavender	Sandalwood
Lemon	Wintergreen

© Frances Stein

The sharp, spicy aroma of rosemary is especially suitable in winter, herbal, and Christmas blends.

© John A. Lynch/Photo/Nats

Peppermint has a brisk, refreshing fragrance that is enjoyed by almost everyone.

KITCHEN METRICS

For cooking and baking convenience, use the following metric measurements:

SPOONS:

1/4 teaspoon = 1 milliliter
1/2 teaspoon = 2 milliliters
1 teaspoon = 5 milliliters
1 tablespoon = 15 milliliters
2 tablespoons = 25 milliliters
3 tablespoons = 50 milliliters

CUPS:

1/4 cup = 50 milliliters
1/3 cup = 75 milliliters
1/2 cup = 125 milliliters
2/3 cup = 150 milliliters
3/4 cup = 175 milliliters
1 cup = 250 milliliters

OVEN TEMPERATURES:

200° F = 100° C
225° F = 110° C
250° F = 120° C
275° F = 140° C
300° F = 150° C
325° F = 160° C
350° F = 180° C
375° F = 190° C
400° F = 200° C
425° F = 220° C
450° F = 230° C
475° F = 240° C

WEIGHT AND MEASURE EQUIVALENTS

1 inch = 2.54 centimeters
1 square inch = 6.45 square centimeters
1 foot = .3048 meters
1 square foot = 929.03 square centimeters
1 yard = .9144 meters
1 square yard = .84 square meters
1 ounce = 28.35 grams
1 pound = 453.59 grams

INDEX